How to Use This Book

Look for these special features in this book:

SIDEBARS, **CHARTS**, **GRAPHS**, and original **MAPS** expand your understanding of what's being discussed—and also make useful sources for class-room reports.

FAQs answer common **F**requently **A**sked **Q**uestions about people, places, and things.

WOW FACTORS offer "Who knew?" facts to keep you thinking.

TRAVEL GUIDE gives you tips on exploring the state—either in person or right from your chair!

PROJECT ROOM provides fun ideas for school assignments and incredible research projects. Plus, there's a guide to primary sources—what they are and how to cite them.

Please note: All statistics are as up-to-date as possible at the time of publication. Population data is taken from the 2010 census.

Consultants: Pamela Bennett, Director of the Indiana Historical Bureau; Jeremy D. Dunning, Professor of Geophysics, Indiana University; William Loren Katz; Dawn E. Bakken, Associate Editor, *Indiana Magazine of History*

Book production by The Design Lab

Library of Congress Cataloging-in-Publication Data
Stille, Darlene R.
 Indiana / by Darlene R. Stille. — Revised edition.
 pages cm. — (America the beautiful. Third series)
 Includes bibliographical references and index.
 ISBN 978-0-531-24884-3 (lib. bdg.)
 1. Indiana—Juvenile literature. I. Title.
 F526.3.S75 2014
 977.2—dc23   2013031926

1 2 3 4 5 6 7 8 9 10 R 23 22 21 20 19 18 17 16 15 14

AMERICA ★ THE ★ BEAUTIFUL

Indiana

BY DARLENE R. STILLE

Third Series, Revised Edition

Children's Press®
An Imprint of Scholastic Inc.
New York ★ Toronto ★ London ★ Auckland ★ Sydney
Mexico City ★ New Delhi ★ Hong Kong
Danbury, Connecticut

CONTENTS

1 LAND

Glaciers and other earth-changing events lead to sandy dunes, rich soil, and lakes and rivers. **8**

2 FIRST PEOPLE

Ancient builders of mounds and pyramids create a great city, then disappear mysteriously. Algonquian groups follow. **24**

3 EXPLORATION AND SETTLEMENT

The French seek to live peacefully with Native Americans, but the British do not, as both struggle for control of the continent. Americans capture British forts, ensuring that Indiana will be part of the United States. **32**

6 PEOPLE

Amish quilts and Indy race cars, basketball and poetry—all these aspects of Indiana culture enrich the world. **66**

7

From the state capitol to the smallest town hall, all Indianans can have a say in how their government works. **80**

8 GOVERNMENT · ECONOMY

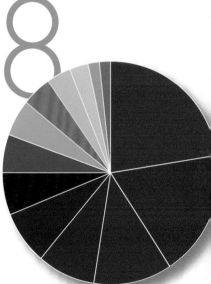

Indiana farms, factories, and foundries all contribute to the economy. **94**

GROWTH AND CHANGE

4

Automobiles and railroads combine to make Indiana a giant of industry and "the Crossroads of America." **42**

MORE MODERN TIMES

5

With the tremendous output of Indiana industries, the United States contributes to the Allied victory in World War II. In the second part of the century, Indiana learns to meet the challenges of changing times. **56**

9 TRAVEL GUIDE

Climb a sand dune, explore a cave, watch a car race, or step back in time at a living history museum— you can do it all in Indiana. **102**

PROJECT ROOM

★

PROJECTS. 116

TIMELINE 122

GLOSSARY 125

FAST FACTS 126

BIOGRAPHICAL DICTIONARY. . .133

RESOURCES 138

★

INDEX 139

AUTHOR'S TIPS AND
SOURCE NOTES. 143

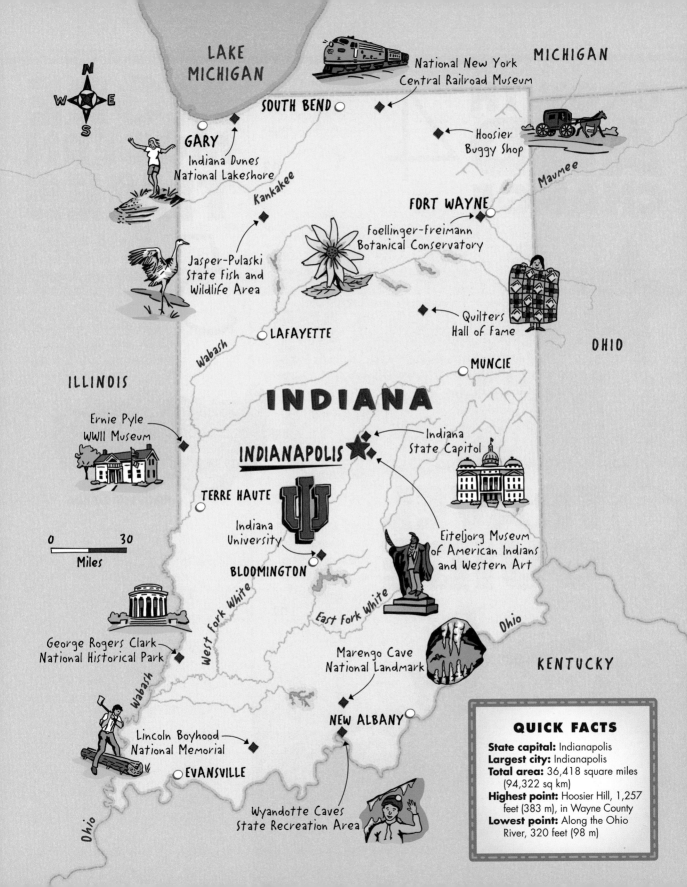

LAKE MICHIGAN

MICHIGAN

National New York Central Railroad Museum

Hoosier Buggy Shop

SOUTH BEND

GARY

Indiana Dunes National Lakeshore

Kankakee

Maumee

FORT WAYNE

Foellinger-Freimann Botanical Conservatory

Jasper-Pulaski State Fish and Wildlife Area

Quilters Hall of Fame

LAFAYETTE

Wabash

OHIO

ILLINOIS

MUNCIE

INDIANA

Ernie Pyle WWII Museum

INDIANAPOLIS

Indiana State Capitol

TERRE HAUTE

Indiana University

Eiteljorg Museum of American Indians and Western Art

BLOOMINGTON

West Fork White

East Fork White

Ohio

George Rogers Clark National Historical Park

Marengo Cave National Landmark

KENTUCKY

Wabash

NEW ALBANY

Lincoln Boyhood National Memorial

EVANSVILLE

Ohio

Wyandotte Caves State Recreation Area

QUICK FACTS

State capital: Indianapolis
Largest city: Indianapolis
Total area: 36,418 square miles (94,322 sq km)
Highest point: Hoosier Hill, 1,257 feet (383 m), in Wayne County
Lowest point: Along the Ohio River, 320 feet (98 m)

Welcome to Indiana!

HOW DID INDIANA GET ITS NAME?

INDIANA

Indiana means "land of the Indians," but the name was originally applied to a place different from the state of Indiana. British traders in the 1760s gave this name to some land farther east that they had received from Native Americans. Virginia, however, claimed to own the land and added the first "Indiana" to its territory. After the Revolutionary War, the new United States named the land west of the Ohio River the Indiana Territory. When new states were carved from this territory, one of them was named Indiana.

8

READ ABOUT

Prehistoric
Ice 11

Land
Regions 12

Climate. 14

Plant Life 16

Animal Life . . . 17

Humans and the
Environment. . . 18

Mount Baldy, a
dune in Indiana
Dunes National
Lakeshore

LAND

★

IN INDIANA, SAND DUNES LINE THE LAKE MICHIGAN SHORE, AND IN THE CENTER OF THE STATE, FIELDS OF CORN AND SOYBEANS STRETCH TO THE HORIZON. The southern end of the state boasts steep hills and limestone caves. Overall, the 36,418 square miles (94,322 square kilometers) that make up Indiana are pretty level. The highest point, in Wayne County along the Ohio border, is Hoosier Hill at 1,257 feet (383 meters) above sea level. The lowest point, in the southwest where the Wabash River flows into the Ohio River, is 320 feet (98 m) above sea level.

Indiana Topography

Use the color-coded elevation chart to see on the map Indiana's high points (orange) and low points (green to dark green). Elevation is measured as the distance above or below sea level.

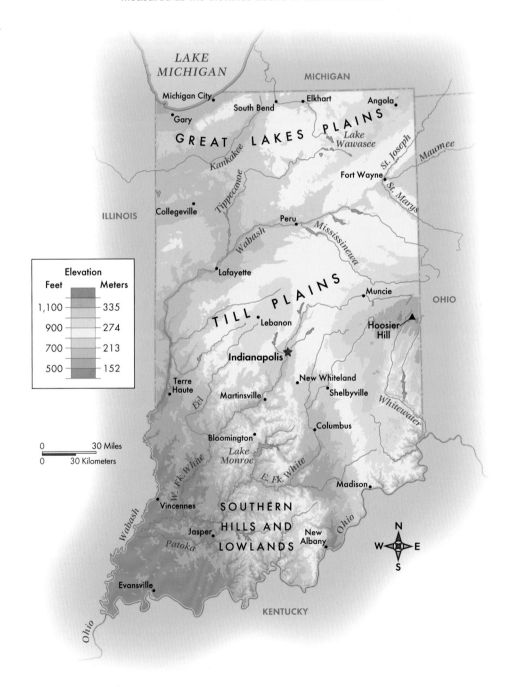

PREHISTORIC ICE

Indianans can thank prehistoric ice sheets called glaciers for making much of their state look the way it does today. Ice covered Indiana as far south as Martinsville several times in the distant past. The last ice age in Indiana began about 700,000 years ago. As the climate became colder, ice crept slowly south from what is now Michigan to where Indianapolis is today. When the climate warmed, the glaciers **receded**. The last ice age ended in Indiana 10,000 to 12,000 years ago.

The glaciers made drastic changes to the land. The ice mowed down forests and rocky hills. It pushed dirt and gravel into river gorges and valleys. It ground up rocks that would become rich soil. The glaciers and melting ice created Lake Michigan, one of the five Great Lakes, and smaller lakes and rivers in Indiana. The largest of these smaller lakes is Lake Wawasee between South Bend and Fort Wayne.

Earthquakes in Indiana? They happen once in a while. A 1909 quake between Terre Haute and Vincennes knocked down chimneys and shook pictures from walls.

WORD TO KNOW

receded *pulled or moved back over time*

Indiana Geo-Facts

Along with the state's geographical highlights, this chart ranks Indiana's land, water, and total area compared to all other states.

Total area; rank . . . . 36,418 square miles (94,322 sq km); 38th
    Land; rank . . . . 35,867 square miles (92,895 sq km); 38th
    Water; rank . . . . 551 square miles (1,427 sq km); 39th
    Inland water; rank . . . . .316 square miles (818 sq km); 43rd
    Great Lakes; rank . . . . 235 square miles (609 sq km); 8th
Geographic center . . . . Boone County, 14 miles (23 km)
                                                        north-northwest of Indianapolis
Latitude . . . . 37° 47' N to 41° 46' N
Longitude. . . . . 84° 49' W to 88° 4' W
Highest point . . . . Hoosier Hill, 1,257 feet (383 m), in Wayne County
Lowest point . . . . .Along the Ohio River, 320 feet (98 m)
Largest city . . . . Indianapolis
Longest river .Wabash, 475 miles (764 km)

Rhode Island, the nation's smallest state, would fit inside Indiana 23 times!

Corn is harvested on an Indiana farm.

LAND REGIONS

Four states and Lake Michigan border Indiana. Michigan and Lake Michigan are to the north. Ohio is to the east. The Ohio River separates Indiana from Kentucky, the state to its south. The Wabash River separates Indiana from Illinois, the state to its west. Within Indiana lie three main land regions: The Great Lakes Plains, the Till Plains, and the Southern Hills and Lowlands.

The Great Lakes Plains

The Great Lakes Plains form a strip of fertile lowland across northern Indiana that also stretches across southern Michigan, northern Illinois, southern Wisconsin, and into northwest Ohio. In the central Great Lakes

Plains, glaciers left behind many small lakes, ridges, and small hills called drumlins. The rich soil in the southern part of Indiana's Great Lakes Plains makes good farmland.

The Till Plains

The Till Plains are a band of deep, rich soil across the center of Indiana, beginning in Kansas and Nebraska and stretching to western Ohio. Indiana's Till Plains seem almost flat.

The Southern Hills and Lowlands

The Southern Hills and Lowlands are in south-central Indiana. Glaciers never arrived to grind down this part of the state, which has more hills and valleys than any other part of Indiana. Underground streams have carved out several caves. The soil in the Southern Hills and Lowlands is not as rich as in other parts of Indiana. But the area does have deposits of coal and oil.

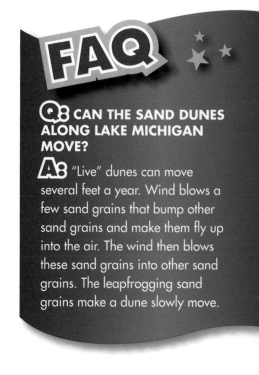

FAQ

Q8 CAN THE SAND DUNES ALONG LAKE MICHIGAN MOVE?

A8 "Live" dunes can move several feet a year. Wind blows a few sand grains that bump other sand grains and make them fly up into the air. The wind then blows these sand grains into other sand grains. The leapfrogging sand grains make a dune slowly move.

A waterfall at McCormick's Creek State Park

Hoosiers shovel out after a snowstorm in Carmel.

CLIMATE

All of Indiana has a moderate climate, but the weather can be very different in the northern and southern parts of the state. Warm, moist air blows up from the Gulf of Mexico to help make the southern parts of Indiana warmer than the northern parts. Summer days in Evansville in the south are hot and humid. Evansville's average daily high temperature in July is 89 degrees Fahrenheit (32 degrees Celsius). South Bend in the north has a lower average daily high in July of 83°F (28°C).

Winters tend to be more severe in the north. Evansville, in the south, might get 13 inches (33 centimeters) of snow in a year, while Michigan City on Lake Michigan can get more than 20 inches (51 cm) in just a day or two. As cold air passes over the warmer waters of the big lake, it makes the water evaporate, forming clouds that drop snow along the shore. Strong winds can blow these "lake effect" snow clouds from Gary to South Bend and even to Elkhart. In the plains area of Indiana, powerful thunderstorms can flare up in the spring and summer.

TRAGIC TORNADOES

Indiana is on the edge of what is called "tornado alley," a region that is mainly in the Great Plains states. Warm, moist air blowing over the flat plains from the Gulf of Mexico sometimes collides with cold dry air coming down from the Arctic. Thunderstorms fire up where the two air masses meet. In the most powerful thunderstorms, winds start to swirl and form a funnel—a tornado. Sometimes the tornado touches down on the ground and, like a giant vacuum cleaner, it can suck up cars, tear off roofs, and flatten houses.

FLOODS

Heavy rains sometimes cause Indiana rivers to flood. Indiana's worst flooding occurred in 1913 along the Whitewater River, a **tributary** of the Miami River in Ohio. Between 5 and 9 inches (13 and 23 cm) of rain and sleet fell during two days in March. Some 90 people died as a result of the flood. Flooding along the Ohio River in 1937 also caused great damage to Indiana towns along the river from the Ohio border to Illinois.

WORD TO KNOW

tributary *a smaller river that flows into a larger river*

A homeowner sorts through the wreckage after a tornado in Marysville on March 4, 2012.

Weather Report

This chart shows record temperatures (high and low) for the state, as well as average temperatures (July and January) and average annual precipitation for Indiana.

Record high temperature . . . . 116°F (47°C) at Collegeville
on July 14, 1936
Record low temperature . . . . –36°F (–38°C) at New Whiteland
on January 19, 1994
Average July temperature, Indianapolis . . . . .74°F (23°C)
Average January temperature, Indianapolis . . . . 26°F (–3°C)
Average yearly precipitation, Indianapolis . . . . .40 inches (102 cm)

Source: National Climatic Data Center, NESDIS, NOAA, U.S. Department of Commerce

Indiana's most destructive tornadoes to date struck the northern and central parts of the state in April 1965. Eleven tornadoes touched down in 20 counties. Swirling winds and flying debris killed 137 people and injured more than 1,700 others.

PLANT LIFE

Many of the plants found in Indiana are the kinds seen in most midwestern fields, forests, and backyards. Oak, maple, black walnut, hickory, ash, beech, elm, and sycamore trees grow in the forests that cover about one-fifth of the state. Prairie wildflowers of central Indiana include milkweed, aster, sunflowers, and black-eyed Susans. Plants more typical of a warm, wet climate grow in extreme southern Indiana, where bald cypresses tower more than 100 feet (30 m) above the water of Goose Pond and Twin Swamps Nature

Sunflower

Grasses grow along a pond at Hoosier National Forest.

Preserve in Posey County. Insect-eating plants, such as the pitcher plant, grow in bogs and other wetlands all over the state.

ANIMAL LIFE

From swampy lands near the Ohio River to windblown beaches along Lake Michigan, Indiana is home to all kinds of wildlife. Rainbow trout flash through inland streams. Perch, bass, catfish, and sunfish fill Indiana's

More than 1,100 native plants live among the sand dunes of Indiana's Lake Michigan shore.

Many river otters make their home in Indiana's wooded areas.

ENDANGERED ANIMALS

Indiana wildlife specialists are working hard to save the state's endangered animals. Among the animals in danger are the Karner blue butterfly, the Indiana bat, the eastern puma, and the piping plover. Bald eagles, peregrine falcons, and river otters once faced extinction. Indiana biologists have had success breeding these animals in captivity and then releasing them back to their natural habitats in Indiana.

many lakes. Squirrels, raccoons, otters, mink, and badgers share the wooded areas with deer. Birds such as cardinals, sparrows, finches, and woodpeckers perch on trees and soar through the skies. In harvested fields, wild turkeys, pheasants, and grouse peck at leftover grain in the fall.

HUMANS AND THE ENVIRONMENT

The growth of industry that brought jobs to Indiana in the late 19th century also caused lasting problems. To this day, coal-burning factories and power plants around Indianapolis and other cities continue to cause air pollution. Steel mills, oil refineries, and factories along

Karner blue butterfly

Lake Michigan and rivers leading to the lake produce large amounts of mercury and other dangerous chemicals. Some of these chemicals are dumped into the lake. Since about 1990, the state has done a lot to clean up the steel mill areas. But Indianans continue to struggle with balancing the need to protect the environment against the need of industry to produce profits and create jobs.

THINK ABOUT IT!

Pollution

Despite Indiana's recent efforts to clean up its environment, the state ranks as one of the nation's worst offenders in terms of air and water pollution. A report released in 2011 by the Natural Resources Defense Council, an international environmental organization, ranked Indiana sixth in the nation for the most toxic air pollution. In 2009, coal-fired and oil-fired power plants emitted about 26.8 million pounds (12.2 million kilograms) of harmful toxins. These included mercury, sulfur dioxide, and nitrogen dioxide. Indiana accounted for 7 percent of the total amount of air pollution from power plants in the United States. In a report from Environment America, a federation of environmental organizations, Indiana ranked worst among the states in water pollution. More than 27 million pounds (12.2 million kg) of pollutants were dumped into the state's rivers and streams in 2010.

Power plants in Indiana are investing hundreds of millions of dollars in facilities and equipment that will reduce harmful emissions into the air and waterways. Hoosier Energy, one of the state's leading energy providers, produces about 20 percent more power today than it did 10 years ago. The good news is that modern, upgraded equipment has reduced emissions by about 55 percent. It's a positive trend that Indiana residents hope will continue.

Land is cleared to build housing developments such as this one in Noblesville.

WORD TO KNOW

urban sprawl *the spread of a city and its suburbs into rural areas*

Another environmental challenge that Hoosiers must deal with is **urban sprawl**. This spread of housing developments, industry, and shopping centers into rural areas chops up large areas of land into smaller areas. Plants and wildlife need a certain amount of space in order to live, but sprawl has broken up the land into areas that may be too small for wild plants and animals to survive.

SAVING THE DUNES

Sprawl and pollution have long threatened the dunes along Lake Michigan. The struggle to save the dunes began in the late 1800s, when steel mills and factories first brought wealth and jobs to the area. As a result of the development, however, many dunes were destroyed.

Indiana made a small part of the dunes a state park in 1926, but soon companies wanted to build more steel mills around the park. Many people worked to stop them, including schoolteacher Dorothy Richard Buell, who organized people to buy

A view of a factory from the beach at the Indiana Dunes National Lakeshore

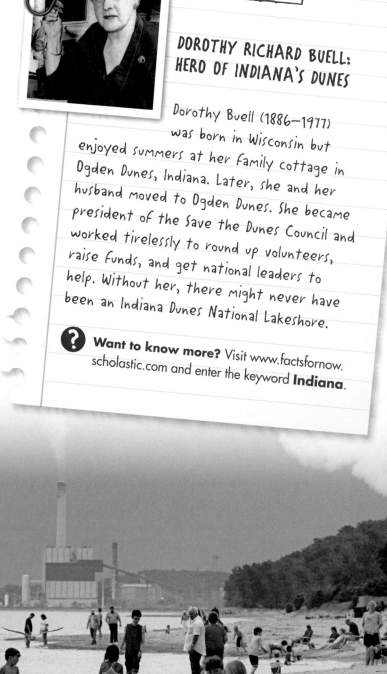

MINI-BIO

DOROTHY RICHARD BUELL: HERO OF INDIANA'S DUNES

Dorothy Buell (1886–1977) was born in Wisconsin but enjoyed summers at her family cottage in Ogden Dunes, Indiana. Later, she and her husband moved to Ogden Dunes. She became president of the Save the Dunes Council and worked tirelessly to round up volunteers, raise funds, and get national leaders to help. Without her, there might never have been an Indiana Dunes National Lakeshore.

❓ **Want to know more?** Visit www.factsfornow. scholastic.com and enter the keyword **Indiana**.

Indiana National Park Areas

This map shows some of Indiana's national parks, monuments, preserves, and other areas protected by the National Park Service.

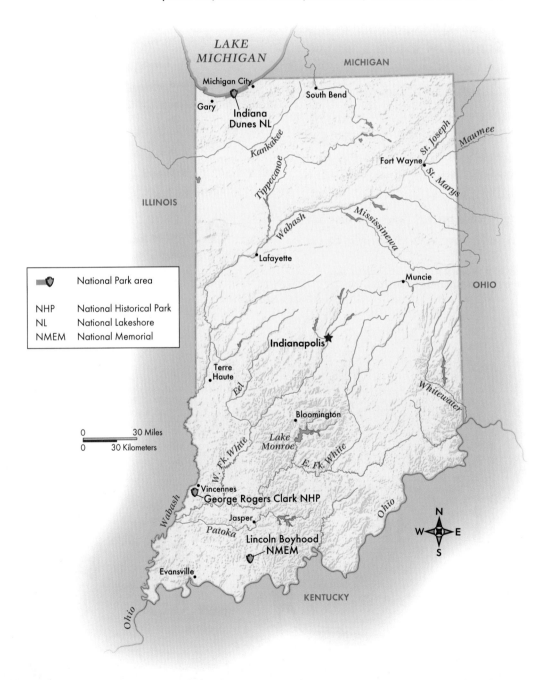

LAKE MICHIGAN

MICHIGAN

Michigan City

Gary

South Bend

Indiana Dunes NL

Kankakee

Tippecanoe

St. Joseph

Maumee

Fort Wayne

St. Marys

ILLINOIS

Wabash

Mississinewa

Lafayette

Muncie

OHIO

National Park area

NHP   National Historical Park
NL   National Lakeshore
NMEM National Memorial

Indianapolis

Terre Haute

Eel

Whitewater

Bloomington

Lake Monroe

0   30 Miles
0   30 Kilometers

W. Fk. White

E. Fk. White

Vincennes
George Rogers Clark NHP

Jasper

Patoka

Ohio

Lincoln Boyhood NMEM

Wabash

Evansville

N
W   E
S

KENTUCKY

Ohio

land around the park. She also convinced national leaders, such as U.S. senator Paul H. Douglas, that the dunes should be saved.

In a 1959 speech, Douglas said, "I can only emphasize that if these mills are built here, with the industrial city that will grow up around them, not only will the Dunes be destroyed, but the little state park will itself be made virtually unusable because of the pollution of air and water." Douglas helped get Congress to establish the Indiana Dunes National Lakeshore between Gary and Michigan City, even though he was a senator from Illinois, not Indiana. He saw the dunes as both a regional and national treasure. The national park that Buell, Douglas, and others helped establish preserves 15,000 acres (6,700 hectares) of dune land along 15 miles (24 km) of lakeshore.

SEE IT HERE!

THE SMOKIN' DUNE

From far away, it looks as if smoke is blowing off the top of Mount Baldy, a sand dune in the Indiana Dunes National Lakeshore that is 123 feet (37 m) tall. In fact, the "smoke" is sand that the wind has picked up from the top of the dune. Mount Baldy is a "live" dune that moves away from Lake Michigan at the rate of 4 to 5 feet (1.2 to 1.5 m) each year.

A backpacker sets out for a hike at Indiana Dunes National Lakeshore.

24

READ ABOUT

Ice Age
Hunters 26

Fire
Makers 27

The First Mound
Builders 27

Pyramid
Builders 29

Algonquians . . . 30

Early hunters used spears to kill mammoths and other big game animals.

c. 10,000 BCE
The first people arrive in Indiana

▲ c. 1000 BCE
People in Indiana begin to make pottery

800 BCE
The Adena culture develops in the Ohio River valley

CHAPTER TWO

FIRST PEOPLE

★

ABOUT 12,000 YEARS AGO, THE FIRST PEOPLE ENTERED THE LAND THAT IS NOW INDIANA. Where did they come from? Their ancestors may have crossed a land bridge between Asia and today's Alaska. Later, the waters of the Bering Sea covered the land bridge. These ancient people kept moving south, and some came to what is now the midwestern United States. Scientists call these ice age people Paleo-Indians.

200 CE ▲
People in Indiana begin to hunt with bows and arrows

c. 1000
Mississippians arrive in Indiana

1450
Angel Mounds is abandoned

These archaeologists investigate the discovery of mastodon remains near Hebron.

WORD TO KNOW

archaeologists *people who study the remains of past human societies*

ICE AGE HUNTERS

Not many Paleo-Indians lived in ancient Indiana, and they left few clues behind. **Archaeologists** have found only some spear points, knives, scrapers, and other stone tools along riverbanks.

The Paleo-Indians moved around as they hunted large mammals, such as mammoths, mastodons, and giant sloths. Over thousands of years, the climate grew warmer, and big forests of oak, hickory, and other hardwood trees began to grow. The large mammals disappeared, forcing the Paleo-Indians to hunt smaller game, such as deer.

FIRE MAKERS

About 6,000 years ago, the culture of Indiana's people began to change. A time that scientists call the Archaic period began. Archaic people may have come up to Indiana from farther south. Like the Paleo-Indians, they probably lived in small groups and moved from place to place. But the Archaic people discovered ways to make life better. They found that mussels in the Wabash and Ohio rivers were easy to get and good to eat. Archaeologists have found piles of mussel shells they left behind.

But the real revolution was that the Archaic people learned how to cook food. They roasted meat over a fire and boiled food in pots made of animal skins by heating rocks in a fire and putting the hot rocks into water-filled pots. They also learned to prepare certain foods for winter.

Archaeologists in 2006 found one of their prehistoric "kitchens" at Charlestown State Park in Clark County. In this 4,000-year-old kitchen, the Native Americans made oil from hickory nuts. They crushed and ground up the nuts between big slabs of rock, and then boiled the nuts to get the oil, which they could store for later use.

THE FIRST MOUND BUILDERS

Another time of great progress began about 3,000 years ago, when ancient people learned to make pottery. Beginning about 100 BCE, they lived in villages of 100 to 1,000 people and traded with other Native Americans far away. Archaeologists have discovered 45 sites of ancient villages in what are now Martin, Lawrence, and Jackson counties alone. In these villages, oval-shaped houses made of wooden poles covered with bark and hides were grouped in a circle around a central plaza.

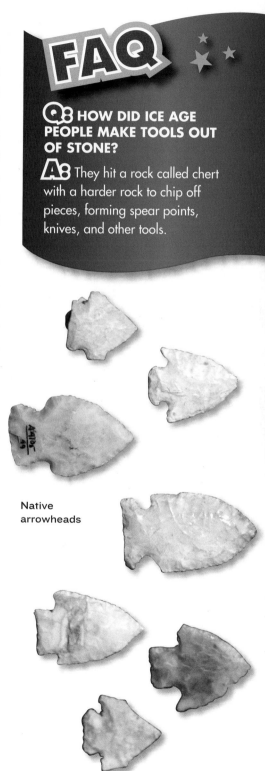

FAQ

Q8 HOW DID ICE AGE PEOPLE MAKE TOOLS OUT OF STONE?

A8 They hit a rock called chert with a harder rock to chip off pieces, forming spear points, knives, and other tools.

Native arrowheads

This painting depicts a harvest ceremony at a Hopewell mound.

Archaeologists have found the remains of dogs in burial grounds, indicating that the Mound Builders kept dogs, perhaps to help with hunting or as pets.

The people also built huge mounds of dirt and rocks. The largest one in Indiana is a circular mound that is 6 feet (2 m) high and 360 feet (110 m) in diameter. Most mounds were for burials, but some may have been places to hold ceremonies. Among the first Mound Builders were the people of the Adena culture, which arose in the Ohio River valley in about 800 BCE. The Adena people built thousands of mounds in Indiana and Ohio. They were mainly hunter-gatherers, but they also grew squash, gourds, and pumpkins.

Meanwhile, another group of Mound Builders came to Indiana from the Ohio Valley around 100 BCE. Archaeologists call them the Hopewell. The Hopewell may have grown out of the Adena culture. The Hopewell people traded with other people far away. They had copper from Lake Superior and seashells from the Gulf of Mexico. They made jewelry and decorated pottery with these materials. The Hopewell people began to disappear from Indiana around 500 CE. What happened to them is a mystery.

Between 200 and 800 CE, people in Indiana began to grow fields of corn and squash. They also learned to hunt with bows and arrows.

PYRAMID BUILDERS

A new group of people began arriving in Indiana around 1000 CE. Archaeologists call them Mississippians. Each Mississippian group had a chief. The chief and other leaders lived in large towns surrounded by fields of corn, beans, and squash. The largest Mississippian settlement in Indiana was at what is now Angel Mounds State Historic Site in Evansville. Several thousand people lived there in houses with walls made of earth and covered with tall, thatched roofs. People of the Mississippian culture also built a number of smaller towns along the Ohio and Wabash rivers.

SEE IT HERE!

ANGEL MOUNDS STATE HISTORIC SITE

What was life like in Indiana's biggest town 800 or 900 years ago? See for yourself at Angel Mounds State Historic Site in Evansville. Archaeologists have been digging up and studying the 500-acre (200 ha) site for about 60 years. Indoor exhibits show how the Mississippian people lived. You can also take a guided hike around the grounds to see models of their earth homes with thatched roofs (below).

Picture Yourself . . .

Living in a Mississippian Town

You live with your parents, brothers, and sisters in a one-room home. All the houses in your village are built around an open area. If you are a girl, you help plant corn, beans, squash, and other crops in the spring. Your mother teaches you how to grind corn in a big wooden pot with a big wooden stick so the grain can be stored in underground pits. She also teaches you how to cook by roasting food over a fire or baking it in underground ovens. If you are a boy, you learn how to fish with nets and hunt with a bow and arrows. Sometimes your family gathers with the other village families in the center square to watch games or see the chief lead a ceremony to mark the change of seasons.

DIGGING UP THE PAST

Glenn A. Black (1900–1964), who was born in Indianapolis, was the first archaeologist to study the mounds in Indiana left by prehistoric people. In the early 1930s, he went to work for the Indiana Historical Society, and he was Indiana's only archaeologist until 1960. He identified or **excavated** about 5,000 sites, including Angel Mounds. When Indiana University established an archaeological laboratory in 1971, it was named in his honor.

WORD TO KNOW

excavated *removed soil and rock from an area to dig up buried items*

Indiana's Mississippian towns were part of a great civilization that began in what is now Mississippi and Alabama and spread north to Wisconsin and Minnesota. In each Mississippian town was a plaza where people gathered for ceremonies. Each town also had at least one earth mound or a pyramid with a flat top. A temple or the chief's house sat on top of the pyramid. By 1450, Mississippians had abandoned Angel Mounds and other sites. Archaeologists are still trying to figure out why the Mississippian culture disappeared.

ALGONQUIANS

Some Mound Builders stayed in Indiana, but they did not plant crops or live in towns. They became hunter-gatherers again.

Soon a few people from the Algonquian group of Native Americans began moving in from the east. The Algonquians were a group of nations including Miamis, Delawares, Kickapoos, Potawatomies, and Shawnees, who all spoke a similar language. They lived in villages, planting crops in spring and summer and hunting animals in winter. Miamis had moved into Indiana to get away from the Iroquois, who attacked them. Miamis were also the first Native Americans in Indiana to meet European explorers, who reached the area in 1679.

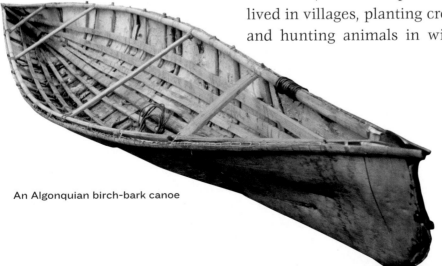

An Algonquian birch-bark canoe

Native American Peoples

(Before European Contact)

This map shows the general area of Native American peoples before European settlers arrived.

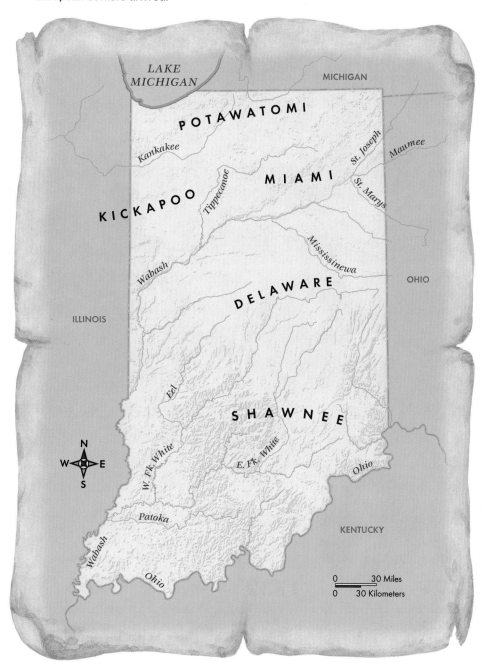

READ ABOUT

The First European
Explorers 35

Indiana's Fur
Trade 36

The British Take
Over 37

Indiana and the
Revolutionary
War 38

French traders came to the region from Canada.

1679 ►
René-Robert Cavelier, Sieur de La Salle, explores northern Indiana

1732
The French found Vincennes, Indiana's first permanent European settlement

1763
The British take over New France

CHAPTER THREE

EXPLORATION AND SETTLEMENT

★

I N THE 1500s, THE FRENCH BEGAN TO SETTLE IN WHAT IS NOW CANADA. They claimed all the land around the Great Lakes for the French king. French explorers crossed Lake Michigan into what would become Illinois, Michigan, and Indiana. Fur traders and priests followed them. French traders offered Native Americans beads, metal pots, guns, and other goods in exchange for the valuable furs. The priests tried to convert the Native Americans to Christianity.

1779 ▸

George Rogers Clark recaptures Fort Sackville

1783

Indiana becomes part of the Northwest Territory

1787

Congress passes the Northwest Ordinance

European Exploration of Indiana

The colored arrows on this map show the routes taken by explorers between 1670 and 1680.

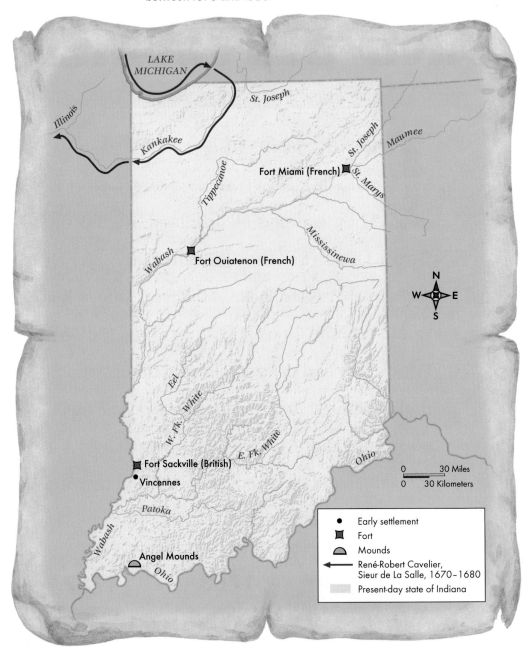

LAKE MICHIGAN

Illinois

St. Joseph

Kankakee

Maumee

Tippecanoe

St. Joseph

Fort Miami (French)

St. Marys

Mississinewa

Wabash

Fort Ouiatenon (French)

Eel

W. Fk. White

E. Fk. White

Ohio

Fort Sackville (British)

Vincennes

Patoka

Wabash

Angel Mounds

Ohio

0   30 Miles
0   30 Kilometers

● Early settlement

▇ Fort

◠ Mounds

← René-Robert Cavelier, Sieur de La Salle, 1670–1680

Present-day state of Indiana

RENÉ-ROBERT CAVELIER, SIEUR DE LA SALLE: DARING EXPLORER

René-Robert Cavelier, Sieur de La Salle (1643–1687), was a Frenchman who sought fame and fortune in Canada. Native Americans told him of great rivers to the south. La Salle thought they might lead to the Pacific Ocean. From there, he could travel to Asia, where he could earn a fortune by trading in silks and spices. He explored what became Ohio, Indiana, and Illinois and traveled the Mississippi River to the Gulf of Mexico. The following year, he tried to reach the mouth of the Mississippi by sea, but his ships landed on the coast of what is now Texas. His crew members ran out of food and water, and many died or deserted. Those who remained killed him because they believed him to be incompetent.

? Want to know more? Visit www.factsfornow .scholastic.com and enter the keyword **Indiana**.

Ships used in the expedition of René-Robert Cavelier, Sieur de La Salle

THE FIRST EUROPEAN EXPLORERS

The first Europeans to see Indiana were French explorers René-Robert Cavelier, Sieur de La Salle, and his expedition of 12 men. He explored northern Indiana in 1679 and 1680. One of La Salle's men described the weather as they traveled along the shore of Lake Michigan: "As we were approaching land our boat was at one time full of water; afterwards it was overset and we lost our entire equipment. . . . For three days we lived only upon acorns which we found under the snow." La Salle and his group paddled their canoes down the St. Joseph River to the south bend in the river. Today, the place where they landed is the city of South Bend.

La Salle claimed Indiana for France, and it became part of a territory that the French called Louisiana. Louisiana also included land from the Great Lakes region to the Gulf of Mexico.

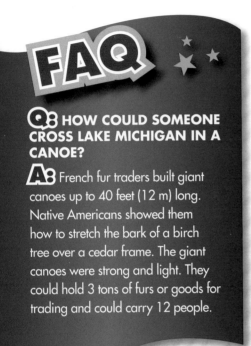

INDIANA'S FUR TRADE

The French began to set up trading posts in Indiana in the early 1700s. The first post was called Fort Ouiatenon (we-ah-tay-NO), on the Wabash River near Lafayette. In 1732, they founded a post farther south at Vincennes, which became Indiana's first city.

Although these settlements were French, people from a variety of races lived and worked in them. The first people of African heritage in Indiana may have been enslaved persons brought in by French fur traders. Slavery was illegal in France, but it was not outlawed in New France. Fur traders owned both Africans and Native Americans. At least one trader was a free, or not enslaved, African. He was Jean Baptiste Point du Sable. In the 1770s, du Sable operated a trad-

Inside a trading post

ing post at the mouth of Trail Creek, in what is now Michigan City, before moving on to what became Chicago.

The French traders and the Native American trappers usually enjoyed a mutually beneficial relationship. French traders often married Native American women and made gestures, such as giving gifts, to show friendship. The traders sold the furs to merchants who made coats and hats for people in Europe, where beaver fur was fashionable. The French became wealthy on the fur trade.

THE BRITISH TAKE OVER

Meanwhile, trouble was brewing between France and Britain, which had established colonies in the East. The British wanted to get in on the fur trade. They were also rivals with France for control of North America. War broke out between the British and the French in 1754. Americans call the conflict the French and Indian War, because many Native Americans were **allies** of the French. The Native peoples who traded with the French allied themselves with the French. In 1763, the war ended in defeat for the French. They gave the British all their lands in Canada and along the Ohio River, including the land that would become Indiana.

The British approach to colonization of land created conflicts with the Native Americans. The British, unlike the French, wanted to take Indian lands, settle them,

Picture Yourself . . .

at Fort Ouiatenon

Your father is a French fur trader. Your mother belongs to the Miami Nation. You live in a log cabin outside a fort at this busy trading post. You play with Indian children in their village nearby. You speak French with your father and Algonquian with your mother. If you are a girl, you do chores around the family's log cabin, helping your mother cook, making clothing from cloth or animal skins, and planting corn and squash in the fields around the fort. Your mother has also taught you to sew pieces of birch bark together to make the outer covering of canoes. If you are a boy, you help your father build the cedar frames for canoes. Later, you will travel with your father to Native American villages to trade for furs.

Replica of Fort Ouiatenon

WOW

New France, the part of North America claimed by France before 1673, extended from eastern Canada to the Rocky Mountains and south to the Gulf of Mexico.

WORD TO KNOW

allies *people who are on the same side in a conflict*

PONTIAC: BRAVE WARRIOR

A leader of the Ottawa nation, Pontiac (1720?–1769) united the Native American groups of the Great Lakes and the Ohio Valley. He led a rebellion in 1763 to get rid of the British, and his Native American forces captured many British forts. He had hoped that France would become an ally and help him fight its old enemy, the British, but the French did not. Pontiac realized that he could not win his war alone, so he made peace with the British. A Native American killed Pontiac at a religious center in Cahokia, in what is now southern Illinois, but no one knows why.

? Want to know more? Visit www.factsfornow .scholastic.com and enter the keyword **Indiana**.

and displace the Indians from them. Native Americans rose up against the British in 1763.

After suffering many defeats by Native Americans, the British government made peace and ordered their colonists not to move west of the Appalachian Mountains. The colonists, however, ignored this order and kept moving westward. To punish the colonists, the British paid Native Americans to raid colonial settlements. The British did not keep control for long, however.

INDIANA AND THE REVOLUTIONARY WAR

In 1776, the American colonies declared independence from Great Britain. In the Revolutionary War that followed, Native Americans in Indiana supported the British.

Virginian George Rogers Clark went on a secret mission to capture British forts in Illinois and Indiana. With only about 200 men, mostly pioneer farmers, he captured forts at Kaskaskia and Cahokia on the Mississippi River in southern Illinois. Most people living at the forts were French and did not like the British, so they did not put up much of a fight. Some went with Clark to capture Fort Sackville at Vincennes. The French at Vincennes also gave up the fort without a fight. Clark left a small number of soldiers at Fort Sackville and returned to Kaskaskia.

George Rogers Clark's troops had to wade through high waters to reach Vincennes.

The British were furious. They marched from Fort Detroit, which today is the city of Detroit, Michigan, and easily recaptured Fort Sackville. It was December 1778, and the British commander let the troops go home for the winter. In the spring, they planned to come back and attack Kaskaskia.

When Clark learned that the British had recaptured Fort Sackville, he did not wait for good weather to return. He and his soldiers set off right away. At some points, the men had to wade through flooded rivers in freezing water that was up to their chests, holding their long rifles over their heads to keep them dry. They ran out of food. After 18 days, they reached Vincennes. They built fires, dried out their clothes, and had something to eat. Now they were ready to take back Fort Sackville.

The surrender of Fort Sackville in 1779

FAQ

Q8 WHAT STATES WERE CREATED OUT OF THE NORTHWEST TERRITORY?

A8 The territory was eventually carved into the states of Ohio, Indiana, Illinois, Michigan, and Wisconsin.

Clark tricked the British into thinking that he had a large army by digging trenches around the fort and by ordering his soldiers to march waving flags and making enough noise for at least 600 troops. The Americans, who were deadly marksmen, shot at the British. Clark also began to dig tunnels into the fort. All of this activity frightened the British into surrendering.

The Americans held the forts in Indiana during the Revolutionary War. Clark's military victories were important contributions toward the Americans winning all the British lands between the Appalachian Mountains and the Mississippi River when the war ended in 1783. The new nation named these lands the Northwest Territory.

The U.S. government rewarded Clark and his soldiers with land in what would become the state of Indiana. The soldiers founded the first American settlement in Indiana, a town called Clarksville. In 1787, Congress passed the Northwest Ordinance, a document that divided the rest of the Northwest Territory into townships and sections. The ordinance stated that as many as five states would be created from the Northwest Territory and that an area could become a state once it had 60,000 settlers.

Arthur St. Clair became the Northwest Territory's first governor, and Marietta, in what is now Ohio, became the capital. When St. Clair arrived in Marietta in 1788, the town faced constant attacks by Native Americans, who had never surrendered the land. St. Clair demanded that the Native Americans give up the entire Ohio Valley. When he tried to bribe Native American leaders, they became enraged. They began to prepare for war.

SEE IT HERE!

GEORGE ROGERS CLARK NATIONAL HISTORICAL PARK

A park and memorial in Vincennes honor the feat of George Rogers Clark in driving the British from Fort Sackville. The memorial is a large, round building. Inside it are seven murals that tell the story of how Clark captured the fort. Every summer, the National Park Service offers rides on the Wabash River in a big canoe, from which visitors can see the fort as French fur trappers did.

The Ohio River near Marietta

42

READ ABOUT

The Final
Battles......44

Settlement and
Statehood....46

Roads and
Railroads 48

The Underground
Railroad and the
Civil War 50

Autos and
Oil........51

Immigration...54

Settlers on the
Wabash River

1795

The Treaty of Greenville
gives lands in Indiana to
the United States

1800

Indiana Territory
is created

1816 ▶

Indiana becomes
the 19th state

CHAPTER FOUR

GROWTH AND CHANGE

★

WITH ALL THEIR BELONGINGS PILED ON RAFTS, COLONISTS POLED AND FLOATED ALONG THE OHIO AND WABASH RIVERS. They came to settle the land of Indiana. Native Americans watched the settlers arrive, fearing that the settlers would take even more land.

1847
Indiana's first railroad is built

1889
Standard Oil decides to build a refinery in Whiting

1911 ▲
First Indianapolis 500 race is held

A scene from the Battle of Tippecanoe in 1811

WORD TO KNOW

confederation *an association of groups that comes together with common goals*

THE FINAL BATTLES

The trouble began in Ohio. A **confederation** of Algonquian groups, led by the great Miami leader Little Turtle, began attacking the settlers. President George Washington sent 1,400 soldiers in 1790 to destroy Indian villages in Indiana and western Ohio. Little Turtle lured the soldiers into a trap near Fort Wayne and defeated them. The next year, Washington sent in 2,000 poorly trained troops, and the Native Americans defeated this force, too.

Finally, in 1794, Washington had General Anthony Wayne assemble an army of 3,000 seasoned fighters. Wayne—who had earned the nickname "Mad Anthony" for his reckless bravery during the Revolutionary War— was ordered to destroy the Algonquian confederation and their way of life.

After being driven back by Wayne's forces when he attacked a fort near the Indiana border, Little Turtle realized the Native Americans could not defeat Wayne, so he urged peace talks. The confederation, however, replaced him with another leader, Turkey Foot, who was willing to fight on. The two sides fought a great battle at a place called Fallen Timbers near Toledo, Ohio, and the U.S. troops overwhelmed the Native Americans. Admitting defeat, 1,100 Indian leaders, including Little Turtle, signed the Treaty of Greenville in 1795, handing most of Ohio to the United States in exchange for other land in the Northwest Territory.

In 1800, Congress divided the Northwest Territory into the Indiana Territory and the Ohio Territory. Vincennes was made the capital of Indiana Territory, and William Henry Harrison became its governor. Following the land acquisition policy of the federal government, Harrison had soon persuaded and pressured Native Americans to sell land in Indiana. He helped make it possible for settlers to buy the land on credit.

A great Shawnee leader named Tecumseh did not believe that anyone could buy or sell land. "Sell a country!" he wrote in a letter to Harrison. "Why not sell the air, the clouds and the great sea, as well as the earth? Did not the Great Spirit make them all for the use of his children?" Tecumseh and his brother, called the Prophet, tried to form another confederation to fight the settlers. Harrison attacked and destroyed their meeting place, a settlement called Prophetstown (near present-day Lafayette), at the Battle of Tippecanoe in 1811.

Tecumseh joined with the British against the Americans when another war broke out, called the War of 1812. Harrison finally defeated Tecumseh's warriors in the Battle of the Thames in Canada. Tecumseh was killed. Almost all the Native Americans then left Indiana. The Potawatomies remained. In the 1830s, they, too, were forced to leave the state.

Tecumseh

SETTLEMENT AND STATEHOOD

New settlers in Indiana Territory came mostly from southern states and Ohio. Rufus Easton, an early settler, encouraged people to come to the new territory, saying "there neither is, nor in the nature of things can there ever be, anything like poverty there. . . . Every person, however poor, may with moderate industry become in a very short time a land holder."

Such descriptions must have sounded especially tempting to African Americans wanting to escape from enslavement in the southern states. The Northwest Ordinance prohibited slavery in the territory. But land speculators and slaveholders asked Congress to change this law and permit slavery as a way of attracting more white settlers. They also flooded the territorial legislature with **petitions** asking that slavery be made legal. Congress and the territorial lawmakers refused these demands.

WORD TO KNOW

petitions *written calls for action, usually with signatures of people who support the action*

A family of settlers in the late 1800s

Indiana: From Territory to Statehood

(1800–1816)

This map shows the original Indiana territory and the area (in yellow) that became the state of Indiana in 1816.

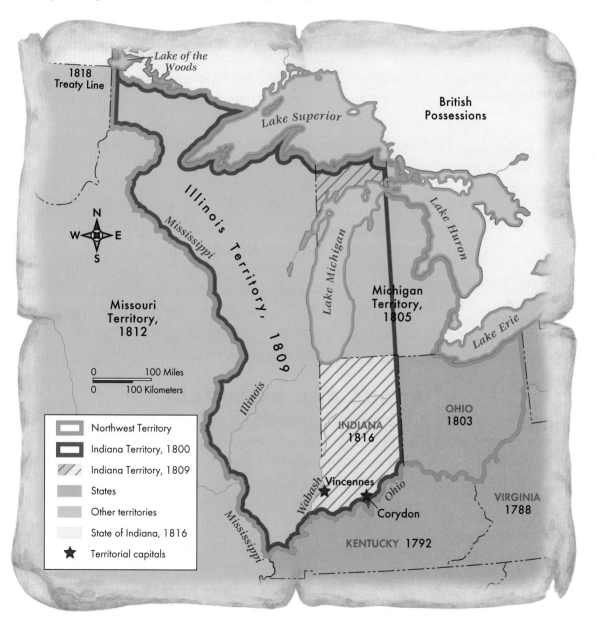

1818 Treaty Line

Lake of the Woods

Lake Superior

British Possessions

Illinois Territory, 1809

Mississippi

Lake Michigan

Lake Huron

Michigan Territory, 1805

Lake Erie

Missouri Territory, 1812

Illinois

0   100 Miles
0   100 Kilometers

OHIO 1803

INDIANA 1816

Wabash

Vincennes

Ohio

Corydon

VIRGINIA 1788

Mississippi

KENTUCKY 1792

Legend:
- Northwest Territory
- Indiana Territory, 1800
- Indiana Territory, 1809
- States
- Other territories
- State of Indiana, 1816
- ★ Territorial capitals

SEE IT HERE!

NEW HARMONY

This village on the Wabash River near Evansville was founded in the early 1800s by a group of deeply religious German Americans called Harmonists, who wanted to create a perfect society through hard work, **frugal** living, and prayer. In 1825, they sold their successful town to a group led by social reformer Robert Owen that believed in social equality for everyone. The second group soon quarreled among themselves, and the community broke up. In the 1930s, the state of Indiana bought the town and turned it into a living history museum. Today, you can see what life was like in the 1800s as a tour guide tells about New Harmony's history.

WORD TO KNOW

frugal *careful with money*

The steam locomotives on Indiana's first trains burned wood and pulled cars that looked like stagecoaches.

Although it remained illegal, slavery did not die in Indiana—it just changed its name. When Governor Harrison arrived in the territory with slaves, he called them indentured servants. These were people who willingly signed on to work for a master without wages, in exchange for food and shelter. Many slaveholders who moved to Indiana followed his example.

In 1803, Indiana became the first territory to pass a law restricting the rights of African Americans. The "Black Law" prohibited testimony by people of color against whites in court. The territory passed additional laws that prevented black men from voting, being elected to office, or serving in the militia.

In 1816, Indiana became the 19th state. Slavery was illegal according to the 1816 state constitution. This document also made the state largely responsible for providing a public education system.

Indiana's first state capital was Corydon, which in 1813 had replaced Vincennes as the territory's capital. But lawmakers had set aside land for a new capital in the center of the state. It would be called Indianapolis, meaning "city of the Indians."

ROADS AND RAILROADS

Indianapolis grew slowly because it was hard to get there. Rivers at that time were the best transportation routes, but the White River flowing past Indianapolis was too shallow for boats. The few roads in Indiana were awful. In some areas, people on foot had to slog through bogs and marshes. Horses and riders could fall into the sticky mud. Wagons and stagecoaches sometimes got stuck in deep ruts or overturned when they hit a big rock or a tree stump.

Things got a little better when the National Road reached Indianapolis in 1831. This gravel road, which

The arrival of a train at the depot in Michigan City

led from Maryland to Missouri, was the first road built with federal funds. Pioneers in covered wagons rumbled westward over the National Road. Some settled on the rich farmlands of central Indiana. In the 1830s, Indiana built the north-south Michigan Road connecting the Ohio River with Lake Michigan, so that these farmers could transport their crops to market.

These early roads still made for slow going. A lawyer who often traveled the Michigan Road on horseback wrote in 1833, "I had many a hard ride with the mud so deep that 15 or 20 miles [24 or 32 km] were a good day's journey." Over time, more and better roads were built.

It was the coming of the railroads, however, that helped Indiana become "the Crossroads of America." In 1847, a railroad with a steam-powered locomotive began operating between Madison and Indianapolis. Soon, seven other major railroads were running through Indianapolis. By 1880, railroad tracks zigzagged everywhere throughout the state.

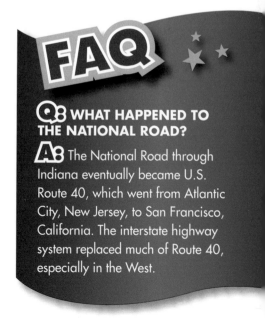

FAQ

Q8 WHAT HAPPENED TO THE NATIONAL ROAD?

A8 The National Road through Indiana eventually became U.S. Route 40, which went from Atlantic City, New Jersey, to San Francisco, California. The interstate highway system replaced much of Route 40, especially in the West.

LEVI COFFIN: ANTISLAVERY ACTIVIST

Born in North Carolina, Quaker Levi Coffin (1798–1877) strongly believed that slavery was immoral and should be ended. Indiana's Underground Railroad received an enormous boost in 1826 when Levi and his wife, Catharine, settled in Newport. They hid African Americans in secret rooms for weeks at a time so that they could rest and regain strength for the journey. During 20 years in Indiana, the Coffins helped some 2,000 enslaved persons escape. The Coffins moved to Cincinnati, Ohio, in 1847 and helped another 1,300 African Americans. Levi's work earned him the nickname President of the Underground Railroad.

 Want to know more? Visit www.factsfornow.scholastic.com and enter the keyword **Indiana**.

WORDS TO KNOW

abolitionists *people who work to end slavery*

secede *to withdraw from a group or an organization*

THE UNDERGROUND RAILROAD AND THE CIVIL WAR

In the 19th century, Indiana's free black settlers faced hostility from many of their white neighbors. In fact, in 1851, the second state constitution barred people of color from entering or settling in Indiana. Other whites, such as a religious group known as the Quakers, were friendly toward African Americans. Some white Indianans were **abolitionists**, people who believed that slavery was wrong and should be abolished.

Thousands of enslaved African Americans bravely escaped from their owners in the South and headed for freedom in Northern states or Canada. It was a dangerous journey. In 1850, the U.S. Congress passed the Fugitive Slave Law, which stated that escaped slaves captured in Northern states would be returned to their Southern owners. Abolitionists developed the Underground Railroad, a system for helping and hiding the runaways. A number of free black and white Hoosiers helped the runaways by giving them food, clothing, and places to hide. "Conductors" guided the escaped slaves from one "station," or hiding place, to another on the Underground Railroad.

By 1860, Southern slave states, afraid the U.S. government would abolish slavery, began to **secede** from the Union. They formed a new nation that they called the Confederate States of America.

When the Civil War broke out in 1861, Indiana sided with the Union, because Hoosiers wanted to keep the United States together. Indiana sent more than 200,000 soldiers of both races to fight. One Civil War battle was fought in Corydon, when Confederate troops crossed the Ohio River from Kentucky. In 1863, these 2,500 Confederate soldiers led by General John Hunt Morgan entered Indiana. Some 450 members of the Harrison County Home Guard failed to stop them. Morgan's Raiders spent six days plundering Corydon and other places in seven Indiana counties. The Raiders finally crossed into Ohio, where Union soldiers defeated them. Over the course of the war, nearly 25,000 soldiers from Indiana gave their lives to preserve the Union.

The Third Indiana Cavalry in 1864

AUTOS AND OIL

When the Civil War ended in 1865, most Indianans, also known as Hoosiers, still made their living by farming. Two developments soon led Indiana to change from a rural state to an industrial powerhouse: the discovery of oil and the invention of automobiles.

The Standard Oil Company discovered oil and natural gas deposits in central Indiana and neighboring Ohio in the late 1880s. The company needed to build a refinery to process the gas and oil into kerosene for lamps and, later, gasoline for automobiles. The refinery had to be close to rail and water transportation.

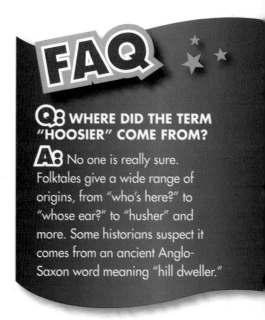

Q8 WHERE DID THE TERM "HOOSIER" COME FROM?

A8 No one is really sure. Folktales give a wide range of origins, from "who's here?" to "whose ear?" to "husher" and more. Some historians suspect it comes from an ancient Anglo-Saxon word meaning "hill dweller."

EUGENE V. DEBS: UNION ORGANIZER

Eugene V. Debs (1855–1926) was a union organizer and founder of the Socialist Party in America. As president of the American Railway Union, he led a **strike** against the company that made Pullman passenger cars. For his role in the strike, he was sent to prison. He ran as the Socialist Party candidate for U.S. president five times between 1900 and 1920. His home in Terre Haute is a National Historic Landmark and a museum.

 Want to know more? Visit www.factsfornow .scholastic.com and enter the keyword **Indiana**.

WORDS TO KNOW

union *an organization formed by workers to try to improve working conditions and wages*

strike *an organized refusal to work, usually as a sign of protest about working conditions*

interurbans *small trains or trolley cars connecting two or more cities*

Standard Oil executives in 1889 chose Whiting, on the shore of Lake Michigan. The lake and three railroads provided easy transportation to the area.

In addition, the location was close to Chicago, the biggest city in the Midwest. Thousands of people moved into Whiting to build and operate the huge refinery.

Nearby, in 1908, the United States Steel Corporation built the world's largest steel mill. The company built housing for its workers and founded the city of Gary. It was named after U.S. Steel's chairman, Elbert Gary. The state made a good gathering place for the key ingredients used in making steel. Boats carried iron ore from Minnesota. Trains brought coal from Illinois and Pennsylvania. Other steel mills and foundries opened in neighboring East Chicago.

Electric train lines were also set up in the early 1900s to carry passengers between cities in Indiana. The trains were called **interurbans**, and they connected Muncie, Terre Haute, Indianapolis, and other Indiana cities and towns. With the coming of the automobile, all the interurbans, except the South Shore Line connecting South Bend to Chicago, disappeared.

Indiana's automobile industry began in South Bend at the Studebaker Manufacturing Company. Studebaker was the world's largest maker of horse-drawn wagons

The first Memorial Day race at the Indianapolis Motor Speedway, May 30, 1911

before it began making electric automobiles in 1902 and gasoline-powered vehicles in 1904. Other automakers set up shop in Indiana. Indiana craftspeople built fine-quality luxury autos and by 1909 produced more cars than any other state except Michigan. Businessman Carl Fisher built the Indianapolis Motor Speedway in 1906, to give pioneering automakers a track to test out new models. It soon became a popular place to hold auto races. The first Indianapolis 500 race was held at the speedway in 1911.

A group of schoolchildren in Gary, early 1900s

High wages paid to maintain the railroads lured many German immigrants to Michigan City in northwestern Indiana in the late 1800s. They earned $1.00 per day.

IMMIGRATION

Between 1880 and 1920, millions of immigrants poured into the United States, looking for jobs and political and religious freedom. They came from Ireland, Germany, Italy, and Mexico, as well as eastern Europe and Asia. They braved long, hard journeys by ship over the Atlantic and Pacific oceans. They flocked to the steel mills, foundries, and factories that were opening up in Gary and other new cities in northwestern Indiana. Most newcomers did not speak English. They were willing to take even the most dangerous jobs.

The population of Indianapolis exploded, from fewer than 19,000 residents in 1860 to almost 234,000 by 1910. Adding to the growth was the migration of African Americans from southern states. African Americans, like members of other ethnic groups, lived together in their own neighborhoods. They formed their own social clubs and published their own newspapers. In 1884, George Knox began to publish the *Indianapolis Freeman* to spread his views on **civil rights** and the duties of citizenship.

The first African American woman millionaire was Madam C. J. Walker, who in 1910 chose Indianapolis as the place to build a factory for making her hair care products. She was impressed with the city's many railroad lines that went all over the country. She was also impressed with the size of its black community.

MINI-BIO

MADAM C. J. WALKER: MILLIONAIRE

Madam C. J. Walker (1867–1919) was born Sarah Breedlove on a plantation in Louisiana. This daughter of former enslaved parents won fame and success by making and selling a line of hair products for African American women. In 1910, she moved to Indianapolis and built her factory there. She was a major contributor to a YMCA for the city's African American youth and to other African American causes. The Madame Walker Theatre Center in Indianapolis is dedicated to African American arts and culture.

 Want to know more? Visit www.factsfornow.scholastic.com and enter the keyword **Indiana**.

WORLD WAR I

Hoosiers again answered the call of their country when the United States entered World War I in 1917. The smoke-belching furnaces and factories in East Chicago, Gary, and Whiting began turning out weapons and vehicles for war. The United States sent more than 4.3 million men and women to fight the war. Almost 117,000 were killed, including about 1,400 from Indiana.

By the time the war ended in 1918, Hoosiers, like other Americans, were tired of the fighting. They were glad to go back to making steel and automobiles and farming the land. They hoped for many years of peace and prosperity.

WORD TO KNOW

civil rights *basic human rights that all citizens in a society are entitled to, such as the right to vote*

READ ABOUT

The Roaring
Twenties.....59

The Great
Depression ...60

Hoosiers and World
War II 61

Postwar
Indiana......62

Indiana
Today.......64

A view of
Meridian Street
in Indianapolis,
early 1900s

1920s ▲
*The Ku Klux Klan is
prominent in Indiana*

1929
*The stock market
crashes*

1933
*One-quarter of
Hoosier workers are
unemployed*

CHAPTER FIVE

MORE MODERN TIMES

★

AFTER WORLD WAR I, HOOSIERS LEFT FARMS TO WORK IN THE GROWING CITIES. For the first time, more Hoosiers lived in the cities than in the countryside. In homes, schools, and businesses, electricity replaced kerosene lamps. With the arrival of electricity came new electric appliances. Soon Indiana became a leading maker of electric stoves, refrigerators, and radios.

1939–1945

Almost 12,000 Hoosiers die fighting in World War II.

1967 ▶

Richard G. Hatcher is elected the first black mayor of Gary

2012

Toyota announces it will expand its manufacturing facility in Princeton

Members of the Ku Klux Klan wore white robes and hoods and terrorized African Americans and other citizens.

WORD TO KNOW

Prohibition *a legal ban on the making or sale of liquor*

THE KLAN IN INDIANA

An increasing number of African Americans came to Indiana seeking jobs during World War I. The Ku Klux Klan soon followed. The Klan was a violent group formed originally in the South to drive former slaves back to white control after the Civil War. In the 1920s, it expanded its hate list to include immigrants, Catholics, Jewish people, union members, political radicals, and those who opposed **Prohibition**.

In Indiana, the Klan claimed to be the voice of American patriotism, and the Indiana chapter became one of the most powerful Klan groups in the country. An estimated 40 percent of white males in Indiana in the 1920s were Klan members. The Klan leader, a wealthy man named David Curtis Stephenson, supported political candidates who helped the Klan take over Indiana politics. In 1925, however, Stephenson was convicted of murdering a woman. After he was sent to prison, the Klan began to lose power in Indiana.

THE ROARING TWENTIES

The 1920s was a time of prosperity for many people in Indiana and all over the United States. The economy was strong. The value of **stocks** was soaring, and some people became rich in a short time. People later called it the Roaring Twenties.

Americans fell in love with the automobile. Wealthy people especially loved the fine cars made in Indianapolis, Auburn, and other towns in Indiana. They rode to picnics at the Indiana Dunes in stately Cole Touring Cars. They drove to Indianapolis offices in Studebakers. They dashed off to football games in South Bend in the sporty Cord or Stutz Bearcat.

Hoosiers listened to jazz, the new rage in music, at clubs like the Black Orchid in Indianapolis. Phonographs and radios brought great jazz musicians such as Louis Armstrong and Fats Waller right into Indiana homes. Hoosiers also loved to see films showing in the big, new movie palaces. They cheered for the Notre Dame football team, coached by the legendary Knute Rockne.

WORD TO KNOW

stocks *monetary investments in a company*

WOW

A top-of-the-line Duesenberg auto could cost as much as $25,000 in the 1920s, compared with a Model T Ford, which cost about $300. In those days, a doctor earned only about $3,000 a year.

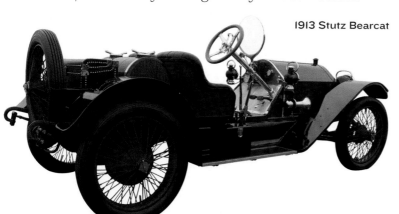

1913 Stutz Bearcat

A team of horses is auctioned off by a farmer, near Montmorenci, during the Great Depression.

THE GREAT DEPRESSION

In 1929, stock prices fell rapidly, and many banks went out of business. Much of the world entered a time called the Great Depression. This era brought hard times for the 3.2 million people living in Indiana. Farmers were especially hard-hit. Prices for farm products had been low during the 1920s, and many Indiana farmers had borrowed money. As prices fell even lower during the Depression, farmers could not pay back the money.

Some lost their farms. Steel mills and factories laid off workers or shut down. Few people could afford expensive cars, so most Indiana companies that made them went out of business. By 1933, about one-quarter of all Indiana workers were unemployed, and many families became homeless.

In 1933, the U.S. government began programs created to help people. One, the Works Progress Administration (WPA), aimed to put Hoosiers back to work. Many Hoosiers worked on WPA projects that improved the state's bridges, roads, and highways. Under other programs, artists painted murals on the walls of more than 40 post offices in Indiana.

HOOSIERS AND WORLD WAR II

The Great Depression started to lift when World War II began in 1939 and the United States began producing war equipment for its allies. The United States entered the war in 1941, after Japanese warplanes bombed the U.S. naval fleet at Pearl Harbor in the Hawaiian Islands. The nation needed soldiers and sailors. It also needed tanks, guns, ammunition, ships, and airplanes. Almost 400,000 Indiana men and women joined the armed forces. Black Hoosiers such as Charles "Buster" Hall joined the Tuskegee Airmen, the first African Americans trained as warplane pilots. Factories and foundries in northwestern Indiana worked around the clock turning out war supplies. Women workers took the jobs of men who went overseas. "I was paid an unbelievable thirty-five dollars a week!" said Virginia Mayberry of Middlebury.

By the time the war ended in 1945, about 400,000 members of the U.S. armed forces had died in the fighting. Almost 12,000 of them were from Indiana.

POSTWAR INDIANA

Hoosiers went back to their daily lives after the war ended. The world was changing, however. Better roads, along with more and better cars, allowed people to live farther from their jobs. Suburbs with new homes and big yards grew up around Indianapolis and other cities. Most people who moved from the cities to the suburbs were white. Meanwhile, African Americans continued moving to Indianapolis, Gary, and other northern cities for jobs. They made up a growing percentage of the urban population. Many African Americans had nowhere to live but run-down neighborhoods. Sometimes, the discrimination they faced led to outbreaks of violence.

Towns such as Elwood, shown here, grew larger after World War II.

A street fair in Gary

During the World War II years, more jobs had opened to people of color, and the number of African Americans in Indiana had doubled. With the increased population came more political power. In 1941, Robert Lee Brokenburr became the first African American to serve in the Indiana Senate. But the big change came in 1967, when Richard G. Hatcher was elected mayor of Gary. Hatcher gained national prominence as a spokesman for urban African Americans.

MINI-BIO

RICHARD G. HATCHER: PIONEERING BLACK MAYOR

Richard G. Hatcher (1933–), born in Michigan City, graduated from Indiana University and Valparaiso University School of Law. In 1967, he was elected the first African American mayor of Gary and one of the first black mayors of a major U.S. city. He won reelection five times and served as mayor for 20 years. After stepping down as mayor, he became an author and college professor.

? Want to know more? Visit www.factsfornow .scholastic.com and enter the keyword **Indiana**.

INDIANA TODAY

Beginning in the 1960s and 1970s, some factories moved out of the state. Many, including the Studebaker Corporation, closed down. Many steel mills in northwestern Indiana closed or laid off workers. The number of steelworkers in Gary dropped from about 30,000 in the late 1960s to fewer than 6,000 by 1987.

Thousands of unemployed whites moved out of Gary, Hammond, and other northwestern Indiana cities. At the same time, the percentage of African Americans in the cities increased. By the 2000s, more than 85 percent of Gary's residents were African American, the highest percentage of black residents of any U.S. city. Many of them were poor and unemployed.

By 2000, some 25 percent of the almost 800,000 residents of Indianapolis were black. Indiana's suburban areas continued to gain in population, mainly as a result of white people leaving the city centers.

Newcomers were still arriving in Indiana during the early 2000s. Many of them came from Mexico, Puerto Rico, and other Spanish-speaking regions. Between 2000 and 2010, Indiana's Hispanic population grew by more than 17,000 people each year. In 2003, the governor's office created the Indiana Commission on Hispanic/Latino Affairs (ICHLA) to ensure economic, educational, and social equality for the newest wave of Hoosier immigrants.

Indiana's auto manufacturing industry was badly affected by an international financial crisis in 2007–2009. In recent years, however, the industry has been making a huge comeback. Indiana has five auto assembly plants, which provide jobs to 600,000 workers. About 14 percent of Indiana's entire labor force works in the auto industry or related businesses. In 2008, Honda

Q8 WHAT IS THE TALLEST BUILDING IN INDIANA?

A8 The 48-floor Chase Tower in Indianapolis, built in 1990 and rising to almost 830 feet (253 m), is the tallest building in the Midwest outside of Chicago.

Inside the Indianapolis City Market

opened a 1,600-acre (650 ha) plant in Greensburg that employs 2,000 people. The plant has provided a boost to the state and national economies: Honda spends about $16 billion per year with parts suppliers throughout North America, many located in Indiana.

The people of Indiana are optimistic about the future. New efforts are being made to protect the environment and the economy is growing. In the summer of 2013, the job growth rate was twice the national average. Employment in the private sector had rebounded to levels not seen since the worst of the financial crisis. Hoosiers take great pride in their state and are determined to keep Indiana the "Crossroads of America."

READ ABOUT

Hoosier
Roots.......68

Indiana School
Days 72

Talented
Hoosiers.....73

Folk Art and Fine
Art.........75

Basketball
and Other
Sports 77

Farmers' markets
are popular
throughout
the state.

CHAPTER SIX

PEOLE

★

HOOSIERS COME FROM A WIDE
RANGE OF BACKGROUNDS AND
CULTURES. Germans are the
largest ethnic group, accounting for almost
23 percent of Indiana's population. The
next-largest groups are Irish and English.
Indiana is also home to people of African
and Hispanic heritage, as well as people
from France, Russia, Poland, and other parts
of eastern Europe.

Indiana Population Growth

This chart shows Indiana's population growth between 1800 and 2010.

Source: U.S. Census Bureau, 2010 census

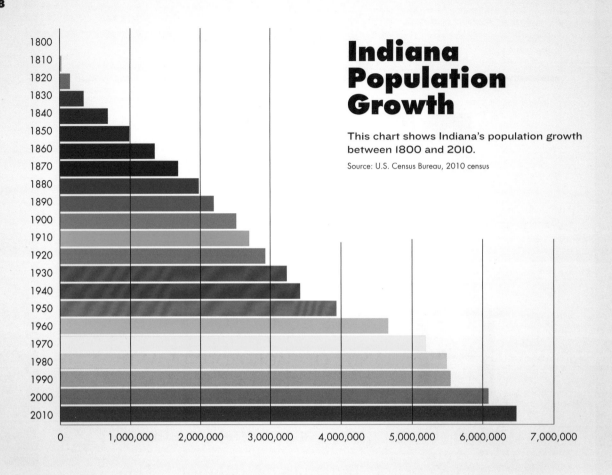

People QuickFacts

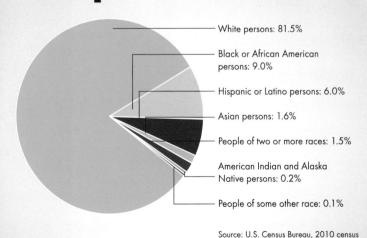

White persons: 81.5%

Black or African American persons: 9.0%

Hispanic or Latino persons: 6.0%

Asian persons: 1.6%

People of two or more races: 1.5%

American Indian and Alaska Native persons: 0.2%

People of some other race: 0.1%

Source: U.S. Census Bureau, 2010 census

HOOSIER ROOTS

People are still immigrating to Indiana. The 2010 census showed that about 293,000 Indiana residents came from other countries. Of these, 15 percent came from Europe, 28 percent from Asia, and 49 percent from Latin America, mainly Mexico. But despite a mix of ethnic groups, Indiana has a smaller percentage of minorities than many other

Where Hoosiers Live

The colors on this map indicate population density throughout the state. The darker the color, the more people live there.

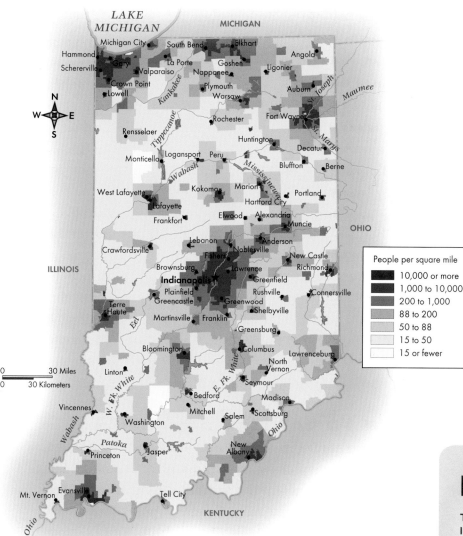

People per square mile
- 10,000 or more
- 1,000 to 10,000
- 200 to 1,000
- 88 to 200
- 50 to 88
- 15 to 50
- 15 or fewer

states. About 82 percent of all Hoosiers are white, compared with about 78 percent for the United States as a whole. Fewer than 10 percent of Hoosiers are black, and 6 percent are Latino.

Big City Life

This list shows the population of Indiana's biggest cities.

Indianapolis 820,445
Fort Wayne 253,691
Evansville 117,429
South Bend 101,168
Gary 80,830

Source: U.S. Census Bureau, 2010 census

JOHN WESLEY POSEY: ABOLITIONIST

Born in Beaufort, South Carolina, John Wesley Posey (1801–1884) helped battle slavery in Indiana. In 1804, his parents came to Indiana, where they freed their slaves. As an adult, Posey bought a farm in Pike County that contained coalfields. He aided runaway slaves by hiding them in the caves and coal shafts. It is estimated that he helped at least 1,000 enslaved African Americans escape from the South. A strong believer in freedom and equality, Posey helped organize the Indiana Anti-Slavery League. During the Civil War, he was a surgeon for the Union army.

Want to know more? Visit www.factsfornow.scholastic.com and enter the keyword **Indiana**.

HOW TO TALK LIKE A HOOSIER

Hoosier is just another word for *Indianan*. Residents call Indiana the "Hoosier State," and they proudly call themselves Hoosiers, a term that has meant someone or something from Indiana since at least 1826. If you run into trouble on the Indiana Toll Road, a Hoosier Helper tow truck is likely to stop and give you a hand.

Some Hoosiers drop the "g" sound on words ending with "ing." For example, a Hoosier might pronounce the word traveling as "travelin." A phrase commonly used by Hoosiers is "half-tempted," such as, "I am half-tempted to go to see a movie." The term means the person is considering something but not fully convinced yet.

HOW TO EAT LIKE A HOOSIER

Hoosiers enjoy corn on the cob, melons, and other fresh fruits and vegetables sold at Indiana farm stands. Pork from Indiana hogs—in the form of sausages or the pork chops sold at the state fair—is very popular. In southern Indiana, Hoosiers love pies made from locally grown persimmons or sweet potatoes. In central and northern Indiana, they savor meat-and-potato dinners as their European ancestors once did.

Watermelon

Corn on the cob

Apple butter

MENU

WHAT'S ON THE MENU IN INDIANA?

★ ★ ★

Fried Pork Tenderloin Sandwich

Many Hoosiers crave this treat. Thin slices of pork tenderloin are breaded and fried, then served on a kaiser roll or hamburger bun.

Amish Apple Butter

The Amish of Elkhart County make apple butter in big iron kettles over a wood fire. The cook peels and cores apples and mixes them with sugar, cinnamon, cloves, and other spices. The apples must be cooked slowly and stirred constantly with a big wooden paddle. Then the mixture gets strained and poured into glass jars.

Elephant Ears and Funnel Cakes

No county fair anywhere in Indiana is complete without these. Elephant ears are made of deep-fried dough covered with sugar and cinnamon. Funnel cakes are made by squeezing dough out of a pastry bag into a vat of hot oil, then coating the curls of fried dough with powdered sugar.

Hoosier Sugar Cream Pie

Sugar cream pie dates back to the 1800s. Pioneer Hoosiers could make it from common ingredients around the house. Layers of butter and brown sugar are spread on a pie crust. The crust is filled with vanilla-flavored cream and baked.

TRY THIS RECIPE
Kettle Corn

Popcorn is very popular in Indiana. It should be. Indiana ranks second in corn production among the states. Plenty of ways have popped up over the years for preparing this snack. Some people like popcorn with plenty of butter. Popcorn balls are popular at Halloween. How about a snack that is both sweet and salty at the same time? Try this recipe for kettle corn. Make sure to have an adult help you.

Ingredients:
¼ cup vegetable oil
½ cup popcorn kernels
¼ cup sugar
1 teaspoon salt

Instructions:
1. On the stove, heat a stove-top corn popper or a metal pot with a tight-fitting lid over medium-high heat. Add the oil.
2. When the oil is hot, add the popcorn.
3. When the kernels begin to sizzle, add the sugar and quickly cover the pot.
4. If you're using a corn popper, crank the handle to stir up the popcorn kernels. If you're using a pot with a lid, shake the pot back and forth.
5. When the popping stops, remove the pot from the heat.
6. Carefully open the lid and add the salt. Lightly toss the popcorn to coat it with the salt.
7. Fill a bowl and enjoy!

Kettle corn

High school art students in Indianapolis work on new designs for a bus stop across from their school.

INDIANA SCHOOL DAYS

Most Hoosier children go to one of Indiana's roughly 2,800 schools. About 740 of these are private schools run by churches or other organizations. The rest are public schools operated by the approximately 300 school districts, which are overseen by the State Board of Education. Students can also choose from more than 50 charter schools, which are partnerships between a local school board and a supporting organization, such as Ball State University. Total enrollment for prekindergarten to twelfth grade in the 2012–2013 school year was 1,041,311. Roughly two-thirds of all Indiana students go on to attend some level of college.

Indiana is the home of several colleges and universities. The music school at Indiana University, based in Bloomington, has produced many musicians and opera singers who have gone on to perform with orchestras and on stages all over the world. More than

20 astronauts or space flight trainees have attended the College of Engineering at Purdue University in West Lafayette. Hoosiers don't have to live in Bloomington or West Lafayette to attend these state-run schools, because there are branches in Richmond, Kokomo, Gary, Mishawaka, Hammond, and many other communities.

Students from all over the world come to South Bend to study at the University of Notre Dame. This Roman Catholic school is ranked as one of the top universities in the country.

TALENTED HOOSIERS

Hoosier writers of note include Gene Stratton-Porter, who set her novel *Freckles* in central Indiana, and Meredith Nicholson, who wrote both poetry and prose. *A Hoosier Chronicle* is one of his best-selling works.

Hoosiers have created some of the best-loved characters in children's books. Hoosier author and illustrator Norman Bridwell created Clifford the Big Red Dog. Raggedy Ann and Andy came from the imagination of cartoonist Johnny Gruelle. Annie Fellows Johnston created the Little Colonel. *Garfield*, one of the most popular cartoon strips of all time, sprang from the drawing board of Jim Davis, who was born in Marion.

PERCY JULIAN: CHEMICAL GENIUS

Percy Julian (1899–1975), who was born in Montgomery, Alabama, did not take his opportunity to study science at DePauw University in Greencastle lightly. He was the grandson of a slave whose right hand was mutilated as punishment for learning to read. Julian went on to earn a doctorate in chemistry from the University of Vienna in Austria. He invented an artificial version of the hormone cortisone—which greatly reduced the price of this drug for people suffering from arthritis—and a drug to treat glaucoma, an eye condition. As a pioneering African American scientist, he served as a mentor and inspiration to the next generation of black students wanting a career in science.

? **Want to know more?** Visit www.factsfornow .scholastic.com and enter the keyword **Indiana**.

WOW

Many U.S. astronauts were born or grew up in Indiana, including Joseph P. Allen, Frank Borman, Ken Bowersox, Anthony W. England, Kevin A. Ford, Virgil "Gus" Grissom, Jerry Ross, Janice E. Voss, Charles D. Walker, Donald Williams, and David Wolf.

Television host David Letterman is joined by his mother, Dorothy Mengering, at the ribbon cutting for the David Letterman Communication and Media Building at Ball State University in Muncie.

MINI-BIO

COLE PORTER: MASTER OF THE MUSICAL

One of America's greatest songwriters, Cole Porter (1891–1964), born in Peru, wrote popular songs with witty lyrics and beautiful melodies. He composed the music and wrote the words to songs for musicals such as Paris and Kiss Me, Kate. His list of hit songs includes "I've Got You Under My Skin," "Just One of Those Things," and "I Love Paris."

? Want to know more? Visit www.factsfornow.scholastic.com and enter the keyword **Indiana**.

Many actors came from Indiana. James Dean, who played restless youths in the 1950s, was born in Marion. Carole Lombard, an early motion-picture star, was born in Fort Wayne. Steve McQueen, a star of the 1960s and 1970s, was born in Beech Grove. TV personality David Letterman and broadcaster Jane Pauley were both born in Indianapolis.

PERFORMING ARTS

Gary gave the music world some of its biggest pop stars in the talented Jackson family. First came the 1970s phenomenon, the group of brothers known as the Jackson 5. Later, several Jacksons became stars on their own, including Michael, who died in 2009, and sister Janet. Other Hoosier music stars include John Mellencamp and Crystal Gayle.

Indiana has outstanding fine arts performers as well. Violinist Joshua Bell was born in Bloomington and has won the Avery Fisher Prize for outstanding achievement. Classical musicians have come from all over the United States and the world to perform with the Indianapolis Symphony Orchestra. Local musicians bring their violins, cellos, and oboes to try out for spots with one of Indiana's several community orchestras, such as the Northwest Indiana Symphony Orchestra or the Richmond Symphony Orchestra. Many communities have youth orchestras and competitions to encourage up-and-coming young musicians. Twyla Tharp, one of the world's most accomplished modern dance **choreographers**, was born in Portland.

FOLK ART AND FINE ART

A Hoosier named Marie D. Webster wrote books in the first half of the 20th century that helped make the craft of quilting popular, with patterns that feature poppies, daisies, tulips, and sunflowers. Her home in Marion became the headquarters of the Quilters Hall of Fame.

Amish women also make exquisite hand-stitched quilts by piecing together fabrics of different colors into geometric patterns with names such as log cabin and wedding ring. A religious group that originally came from Switzerland, the Amish believe in hard work and in living a simple life, shunning such modern conveniences as cars and instead driving horse-drawn buggies. Amish women sometimes auction quilts to raise funds for helping poor people in other countries. Some

Violinist Joshua Bell

WORD TO KNOW

choreographers *people who design the steps for a dance performance*

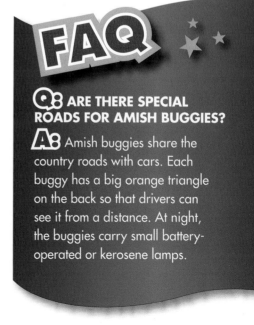

Q8 ARE THERE SPECIAL ROADS FOR AMISH BUGGIES?

A8 Amish buggies share the country roads with cars. Each buggy has a big orange triangle on the back so that drivers can see it from a distance. At night, the buggies carry small battery-operated or kerosene lamps.

An Amish woman sews a quilt.

Amish stitchers sell their quilts in shops in and near Shipshewana. In barns on their farms, some Amish men make and sell wooden crafts, from simple coat-racks to large pieces of furniture.

The Indiana countryside inspired its own kind of fine art painting called the Hoosier School. In the late 1800s and early 1900s, a group of Hoosier School artists painted Indiana scenes, especially in Brown County. They painted in the style of impressionism, which is more concerned with showing light and color than the details of a scene.

Hoosier sculptor Robert Indiana created an image of the word *love* in capital letters with the letter *o* tilted. This image appeared on a U.S. postage stamp in 1973 and was the first in an ongoing series of "love stamps."

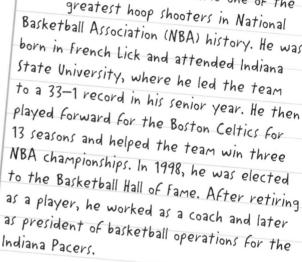

LARRY BIRD: HOOSIER HOOPSTER

Calling himself the "hick from French Lick," Larry Bird (1956–) went on to become one of the greatest hoop shooters in National Basketball Association (NBA) history. He was born in French Lick and attended Indiana State University, where he led the team to a 33–1 record in his senior year. He then played forward for the Boston Celtics for 13 seasons and helped the team win three NBA championships. In 1998, he was elected to the Basketball Hall of Fame. After retiring as a player, he worked as a coach and later as president of basketball operations for the Indiana Pacers.

 Want to know more? Visit www.factsfornow.scholastic.com and enter the keyword **Indiana**.

High school basketball players from Columbus East and South Bend in a state championship game

BASKETBALL AND OTHER SPORTS

If Indiana had a state sport, it would be basketball. You'll find Hoosiers shooting hoops everywhere. This passion for the game even inspired a 1986 movie, *Hoosiers,* about a small-town high school basketball team in 1950s Indiana. The state has produced great professional players such as Oscar Robertson, Shawn Kemp, and Larry Bird. Indiana University former head coach Bobby Knight led the Hoosiers basketball team to 3 NCAA, 1 NIT, and 11 Big Ten championships. Fans also love Indiana's college football teams, especially Notre Dame's Fighting Irish, Indiana University's Hoosiers, and Purdue's Boilermakers.

MINI-BIO

TARA VANDERVEER: HOOSIER STAR AND WOMEN'S COACH

After playing on Indiana University's women's basketball team from 1973 to 1975, Tara VanDerveer (1953–) set off on a career that helped many young women athletes. She has coached women's basketball teams at several universities, including Stanford University. She also teaches and inspires teenage girls at her summer basketball camp in California. VanDerveer has won many honors, including places in the Women's Basketball Hall of Fame and the Indiana University Hall of Fame.

❓ Want to know more? Visit www.factsfornow .scholastic.com and enter the keyword **Indiana**.

Indiana has three professional major league sports teams. The Pacers are the men's National Basketball Association team, and the Fever are the Women's National Basketball Association team. The professional football team, the Indianapolis Colts, won the Super Bowl in 2007 and hosted it in 2012.

Indiana has produced some great baseball players, such as Carl Erskine and Scott Rolen. Other Hoosier athletes include Olympic swim champion Mark Spitz and

Indianapolis Colts fans cheer for their team during a game against the Buffalo Bills on November 25, 2012.

John Andretti in the 1991
Indianapolis 500

NASCAR race drivers John Andretti, Jeff Gordon, and Tony Stewart.

Auto racing is another major sport in Indiana, with more than 50 tracks throughout the state. The Indianapolis 500, or Indy 500, draws race-car drivers from around the world each year on Memorial Day. The 500-mile (805 km) race consists of 200 laps around the speedway. The Brickyard 400 is another popular race. Like the Indy 500, it is held each year at the Indianapolis Motor Speedway.

MINI-BIO

OSCAR ROBERTSON: THE "BIG O"

Oscar Palmer Robertson (1938–), one of the greatest athletes who ever played basketball, was born in Tennessee but grew up in Indianapolis. After college, he played for the Cincinnati Royals and the Milwaukee Bucks and was nicknamed the "Big O." He was elected to the Basketball Hall of Fame in 1979. After retiring from basketball, Robertson set up a variety of companies. In 1997, he donated a kidney to his daughter and soon after became a spokesperson for the National Kidney Foundation.

? Want to know more? Visit www.factsfornow.scholastic.com and enter the keyword **Indiana**.

READ ABOUT

Where the
Action Is 82

The Executive
Branch 84

The Legislative
Branch 84

The Judicial
Branch 87

Local
Government . . . 90

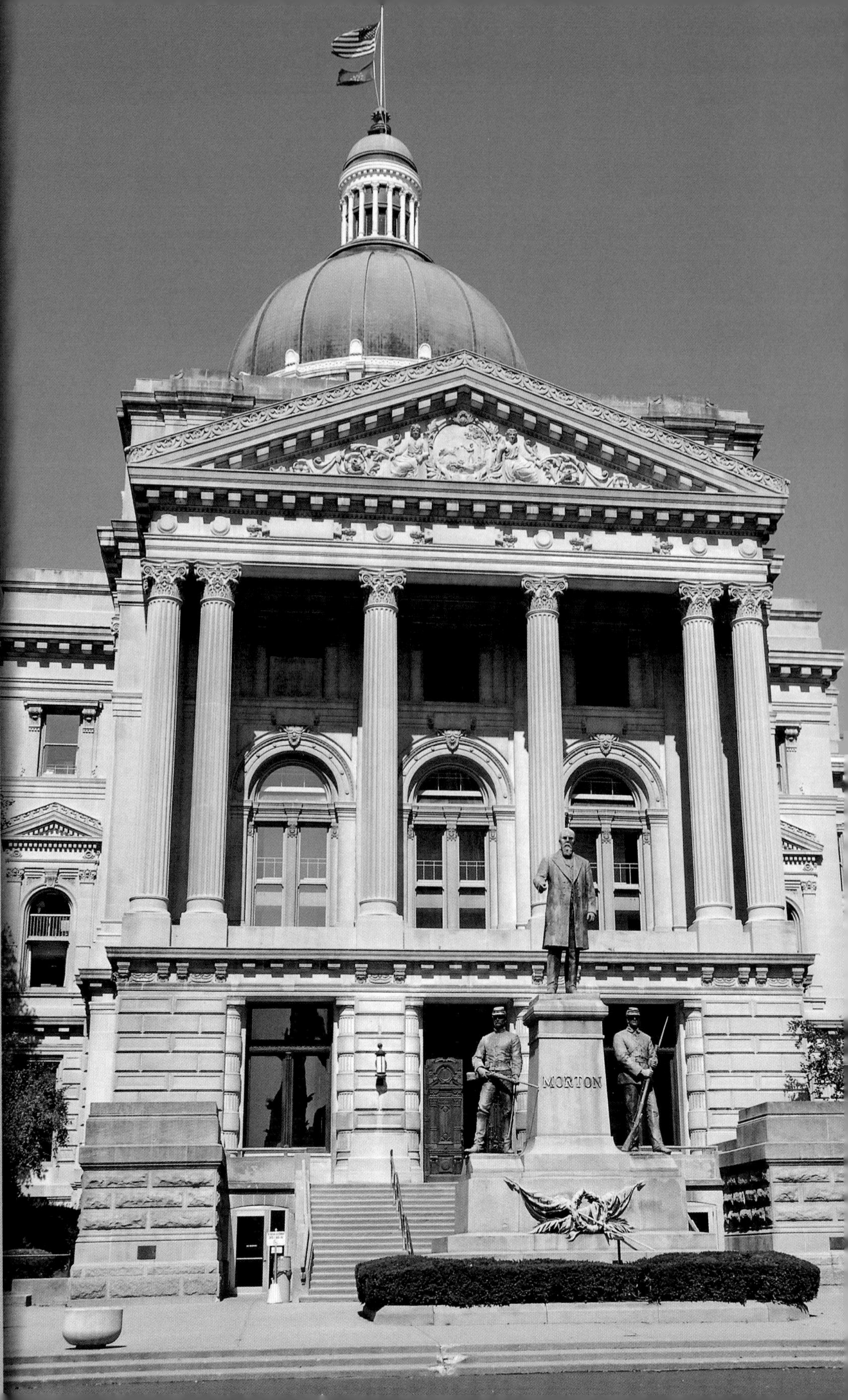

The Indiana
state capitol in
Indianapolis

MORTON

CHAPTER SEVEN

GOVERNMENT

★

HOW DOES INDIANA'S STATE GOVERNMENT AFFECT THE AVERAGE HOOSIER KID? Indiana's government decides how long children should stay in school and how much a family pays in taxes to keep the schools operating. It provides rules for safety at home, at school, at work, and on the highways. The courts help make sure that everyone obeys the laws.

SEE IT HERE!

THE INDIANA CAPITOL

Built in 1888, Indiana's huge capitol is laid out in the shape of a "plus" sign. The building and the grounds around it cover an area equal to two city blocks. Indiana limestone covers the exterior, and the interior is finished with marble and fine woods. A rotunda in the center of the building stretches 72 feet (22 m) across, with a ceiling made of German stained glass. Guides lead visitors' tours almost every day.

WHERE THE ACTION IS

The seat of Indiana's state government is Indianapolis, the state's second capital city. Corydon was the first state capital, from 1816 to 1825. Lawmakers started meeting in Indianapolis in 1825.

Indiana also has had two capitols. The first building was built in the 1830s. It had a poor foundation and had to be torn down in the 1860s. The next capitol had a sturdy foundation of Indiana limestone. Thrifty Hoosier lawmakers, however, wanted the new building to cost

Capital City

This map shows places of interest in Indianapolis, Indiana's capital city.

The capitol in Indianapolis

less than $2 million. When the final bills were paid in 1888, the new statehouse cost exactly $1,980,969.18.

The Indiana statehouse is one of the few state capitols that still contains all three branches of government, although more buildings have been added to house additional offices. Indiana's state government operates from a complex called Government Center, which has three main buildings—the statehouse and two office buildings called Government Center North and Government Center South.

Capitol Facts

Here are some fascinating facts about Indiana's state capitol:

Dome exterior height: 234 feet (71 m)
Number of floors: 4
Length: 466 feet (142 m)
Width: 282 feet (86 m)
Dates of construction: 1880–1888

The state government is set up according to the state constitution. Indiana has had two constitutions. The first constitution was adopted in 1816, when Indiana became a state. The state is governed by the second constitution, adopted in 1851. The constitution calls for three branches: executive, legislative, and judicial.

THE EXECUTIVE BRANCH

The governor is the elected head of Indiana's executive branch and serves a four-year term. He or she appoints the heads of departments and commissions, such as the Bureau of Motor Vehicles, and heads of governing boards, such as the Indiana University Governing Board. The governor can veto, or refuse to sign, bills. The legislature can override a veto with a simple majority vote.

The lieutenant governor takes over if the governor cannot do his or her job. The secretary of state registers businesses and oversees elections. The attorney general, the state's top lawyer, looks after the rights and safety of all Hoosiers. The auditor keeps track of the state's money. The superintendent of public instruction directs the Department of Education, which oversees the public schools.

THE LEGISLATIVE BRANCH

Passing laws that govern speed limits, taxes, and the state bud-get is the job of lawmakers in the General Assembly, which is made up of a house of representatives and

Indiana State Government

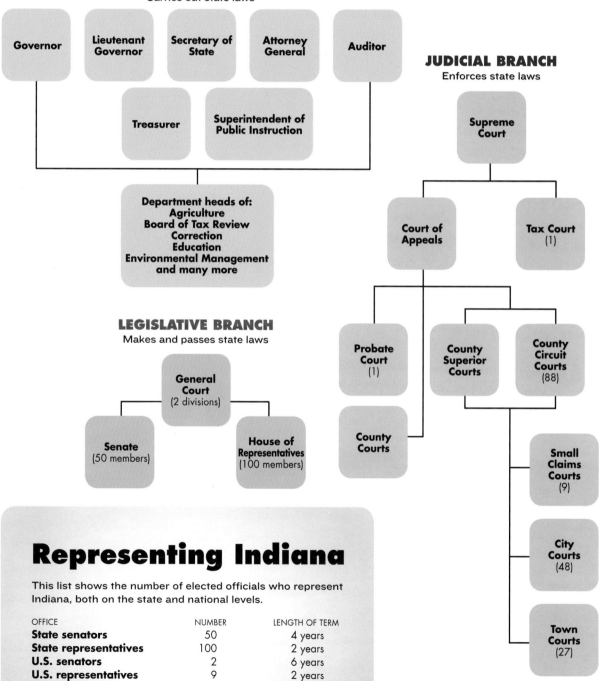

EXECUTIVE BRANCH
Carries out state laws

Governor

Lieutenant Governor

Secretary of State

Attorney General

Auditor

Treasurer

Superintendent of Public Instruction

Department heads of:
Agriculture
Board of Tax Review
Correction
Education
Environmental Management
and many more

JUDICIAL BRANCH
Enforces state laws

Supreme Court

Court of Appeals

Tax Court (1)

Probate Court (1)

County Superior Courts

County Circuit Courts (88)

County Courts

Small Claims Courts (9)

City Courts (48)

Town Courts (27)

LEGISLATIVE BRANCH
Makes and passes state laws

General Court (2 divisions)

Senate (50 members)

House of Representatives (100 members)

Representing Indiana

This list shows the number of elected officials who represent Indiana, both on the state and national levels.

OFFICE	NUMBER	LENGTH OF TERM
State senators	50	4 years
State representatives	100	2 years
U.S. senators	2	6 years
U.S. representatives	9	2 years
Presidential electors	11	—

MINI-BIO

GEORGE WASHINGTON BUCKNER: PHYSICIAN AND DIPLOMAT

Born into slavery in Kentucky, George Washington Buckner (1855–1943) was freed at the age of 10 and later moved to Indiana. There he studied at the forerunner of today's Indiana State University and at the Indiana Eclectic Medical College. After graduating medical school in 1890, he practiced medicine in Indianapolis and Evansville. Buckner's fine reputation earned him the notice of President Woodrow Wilson, who appointed Buckner a diplomat to the African nation of Liberia in 1913. He was forced to resign the position two years later, because he became ill with fever. Today, many of his possessions are on display at the Evansville Museum.

? Want to know more? Visit www.factsfornow .scholastic.com and enter the keyword **Indiana**.

a senate. A new law starts out as a bill in either the house or senate. One or more members from either house can **sponsor** the bill. A bill usually goes to one or more committees that can change it, reject it, or approve it. Once approved, the bill goes to the General Assembly for a vote.

The legislature can also suggest amendments, or changes, to the state constitution. After both houses approve an amendment, it goes to the voters. A majority of voters must approve the amendment before it becomes part of the constitution.

The Indiana house of representatives in session

THE JUDICIAL BRANCH

Since kids are the judges and jurors of tomorrow, the Indiana Supreme Court created a project called Courts in the Classroom to help them understand Indiana's court system. Is a real-life court anything like the courts on TV? What's a **probate court**? What is the difference between a **civil** and a criminal case? Courts in the Classroom answers these and many more questions for Hoosier students in grades four through 12.

Through reenactments of historic trials, field trips to courtrooms, and Web casts and videos of trials, Hoosier kids learn that Indiana has two basic kinds of courts: trial and **appeal**.

WORDS TO KNOW

sponsor *act as a person who proposes or creates a bill*

probate court *a court that deals with wills and the property of people who have died*

civil *involving a dispute between individuals*

appeal *a legal proceeding in which a court is asked to change the decision of a lower court*

FAQ

Q: HOW MANY CASES GO THROUGH THE INDIANA COURTS?

A: All the courts of Indiana handle about 1.5 million cases each year.

MINI-BIO

JOHN G. ROBERTS JR.: CHIEF JUSTICE

Born in Buffalo, New York, John G. Roberts Jr. (1955–) grew up in Long Beach, Indiana, a community on the Lake Michigan shore near Michigan City. After graduating from Harvard University in 1976, he went on to law school. He then went to Washington, D.C., where he worked for Supreme Court justices and U.S. presidents, and became a judge himself. In 2005, he became chief justice of the U.S. Supreme Court.

 Want to know more? Visit www.factsfornow.scholastic.com and enter the keyword **Indiana**.

INDIANA PRESIDENTS

William Henry Harrison (1773–1841) became the first governor in Indiana Territory in 1800 and defeated Native Americans in Indiana at the Battle of Tippecanoe in 1811. Harrison became the ninth president of the United States in 1841, but he died of pneumonia after just one month in office.

Abraham Lincoln (1809–1865) was the 16th president of the United States, serving from 1861 to 1865. Lincoln was born in Kentucky, but his family moved to Indiana in 1816, when he was seven years old. He grew up on a farm near Gentryville. He moved to Illinois at age 21. As president, he led the United States through the Civil War. He succeeded in preserving the Union but was assassinated by an angry Southerner shortly after the war ended.

Benjamin Harrison (1833–1901) was the 23rd president of the United States, serving from 1889 to 1893. The grandson of President William Henry Harrison, Benjamin Harrison was born in Ohio but lived most of his adult life in Indiana. As president, he said that the American flag must fly over all government buildings and schools.

Audience members applaud a speaker at a school board meeting in Gary.

Trial courts hear civil and criminal cases and make rulings. Indiana has four kinds of trial courts. Circuit courts are trial courts that can hold almost any kind of civil or criminal trial. Superior courts are much like circuit courts and can also act as county courts. County courts try cases involving disputes over contracts and lawsuits. They also enforce county laws. City and town courts handle traffic violations and violations of city or town laws.

Indiana Counties

This map shows the 92 counties in Indiana. Indianapolis, the state capital, is indicated with a star.

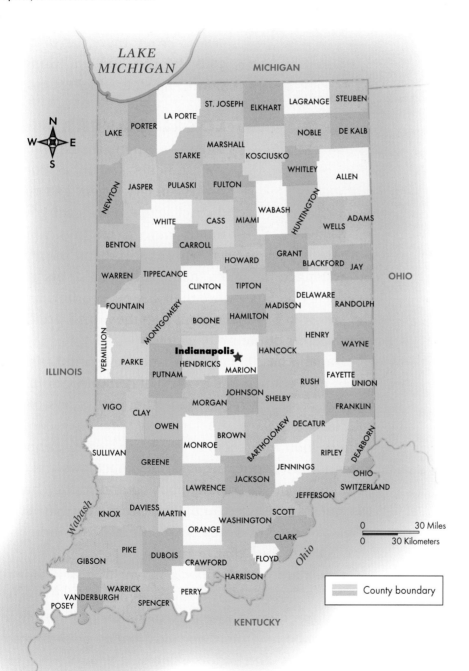

LAKE MICHIGAN

MICHIGAN

N
W · E
S

LAKE

PORTER

LA PORTE

ST. JOSEPH

ELKHART

LAGRANGE

STEUBEN

NOBLE

DE KALB

MARSHALL

STARKE

KOSCIUSKO

WHITLEY

ALLEN

NEWTON

JASPER

PULASKI

FULTON

WABASH

HUNTINGTON

WHITE

CASS

MIAMI

WELLS

ADAMS

BENTON

CARROLL

GRANT

BLACKFORD

JAY

OHIO

WARREN

TIPPECANOE

HOWARD

FOUNTAIN

CLINTON

TIPTON

DELAWARE

RANDOLPH

MADISON

VERMILLION

MONTGOMERY

BOONE

HAMILTON

HENRY

WAYNE

Indianapolis ★

HANCOCK

PARKE

HENDRICKS

MARION

FAYETTE

UNION

ILLINOIS

PUTNAM

RUSH

JOHNSON

SHELBY

VIGO

CLAY

MORGAN

FRANKLIN

OWEN

DECATUR

BROWN

BARTHOLOMEW

DEARBORN

SULLIVAN

MONROE

RIPLEY

GREENE

JENNINGS

OHIO

JACKSON

SWITZERLAND

LAWRENCE

JEFFERSON

KNOX

DAVIESS

MARTIN

SCOTT

WASHINGTON

ORANGE

CLARK

PIKE

DUBOIS

CRAWFORD

FLOYD

GIBSON

HARRISON

Wabash

Ohio

WARRICK

VANDERBURGH

PERRY

POSEY

SPENCER

KENTUCKY

0   30 Miles

0   30 Kilometers

County boundary

HELPING THE HISPANIC COMMUNITY

As the former director of Latino Affairs for the city of Indianapolis, Ricardo Gambetta (1964–) worked to integrate members of the fast-growing Hispanic community into Hoosier life. He was appointed the first director of this agency after Mayor Bart Peterson established it in 2000. Born in Lima, Peru, Gambetta worked as a political adviser to Peruvian government officials. He moved to Indiana in the early 1990s. He became a U.S. citizen and worked as a radio broadcaster and translator. He also helped found organizations such as Hispanic Hoosiers Inc., Indianapolis Latino Expo, and the Indiana Latino Institute.

Only New York has produced more vice presidents than Indiana's five: Schuyler Colfax (1869–1873), Thomas A. Hendricks (1885), Charles W. Fairbanks (1905–1909), Thomas Riley Marshall (1913–1921), and Dan Quayle (1989–1993).

Appellate courts reconsider cases that have already been decided. The court of appeals and the tax court both review earlier cases. From there, any appeal goes to the Indiana Supreme Court, the state's highest court.

LOCAL GOVERNMENT

Indiana has more than 3,000 local governments set up at county, township, city, town, and school district levels. The local governments have a lot to say about how Hoosiers govern themselves. Indiana lawmakers in 1980 made Indiana a "home rule" state. This means that local officials, rather than any other officials, have the power to make decisions that they think are in the best interest of their city or town.

Indiana has 92 counties, and each county is governed by a council and a board of commissioners. The council passes property and other taxes, sets county salaries, and pays the county's bills. The commissioners look after county roads and other property, appoint most county officials, and enact laws and rules involving matters such as housing and traffic control. Counties are divided into 1,008 rural or urban townships governed by a trustee and three board members, all elected to four-year terms.

Cities are governed by a mayor and city council. Towns are governed by a town council, which elects a council president. Cities and towns are responsible for police and fire protection, local parks, streets, water pipes, sewers, and building safety.

These police officers in Indianapolis are some of the many government workers who serve the state.

Indianapolis and surrounding Marion County have a special type of local government. The city and the county merged as of 1970 to operate as the City of Indianapolis.

Indiana's school district governments can pass some taxes and borrow money to operate the public schools. An elected or appointed school board or a board of trustees governs each school district.

State Flag

Indiana's state flag features a flaming golden torch and golden stars against a field of blue. The torch stands for liberty and enlightenment, whose effects are shown in the golden rays that stream from the torch. The outer circle of 13 stars stands for the 13 original states. The five stars of the inner arc represent the next five states to enter the Union. Indiana, the 19th state, is the large star directly above the flame, with the word *Indiana* in a half circle above it. The General Assembly adopted this design in 1917 as part of Indiana's 1916 centennial celebration.

State Seal

The state seal shows three hills in the center, with trees on either side. The sun is setting behind the hills, with 14 rays coming out—13 rays for the original colonies and the 14th representing Indiana. On the right is a woodsman with an axe, and a buffalo jumping over a log is to the left. On the ground are shoots of bluegrass. Above the center are the words "Seal of the State of Indiana," and underneath is 1816—the year of Indiana's statehood. On each side of the date is a diamond with dots on both sides and leaves of the tulip tree, the state tree. The state seal was adopted in 1963.

READ ABOUT

Indiana's Good
Earth 96

Hoosier-made
Goods 99

Motor Sports
Industry 100

Hoosiers at Your
Service 101

A worker at a
Toyota plant
in Princeton

CHAPTER EIGHT

ECONOMY

★

W HEN YOU SEE A MOTOR HOME, TRAILER TRUCK, OR RECREATIONAL VEHICLE ON THE HIGHWAY, THERE IS A GOOD CHANCE IT WAS MADE IN INDIANA. The Hoosier State is a leading maker of all kinds of transportation equipment. Indiana also produces tons of corn and piles of coal. In addition, Indiana is a leading maker of pharmaceutical drugs and medical equipment.

A farmer plows an Indiana field.

INDIANA'S GOOD EARTH

Even though few people work on farms, Indiana's rich prairie soil plays a big role in the Hoosier economy. More than 64 percent of Indiana's land is still used for farming. Indiana is the third-largest among the states in growing soybeans—about 238 million bushels in 2011. Indiana ranks among the top five states in corn production with more than 1 billion bushels in 2007. Indiana is second only to California in producing tomatoes for processing into ketchup and canned goods. Hogs and chickens are the top livestock products for the Hoosier State.

Top Products

Agriculture crops	Corn, soybeans, greenhouse and nursery plants
Agriculture livestock	Hogs, dairy products, cattle, chickens
Manufacturing	Transportation equipment, chemicals, metal products, food and beverages
Mining	Coal, limestone, cement, petroleum

Major Agricultural and Mining Products

This map shows where Indiana's major agricultural and mining products come from. See a cow? That means cattle are raised there.

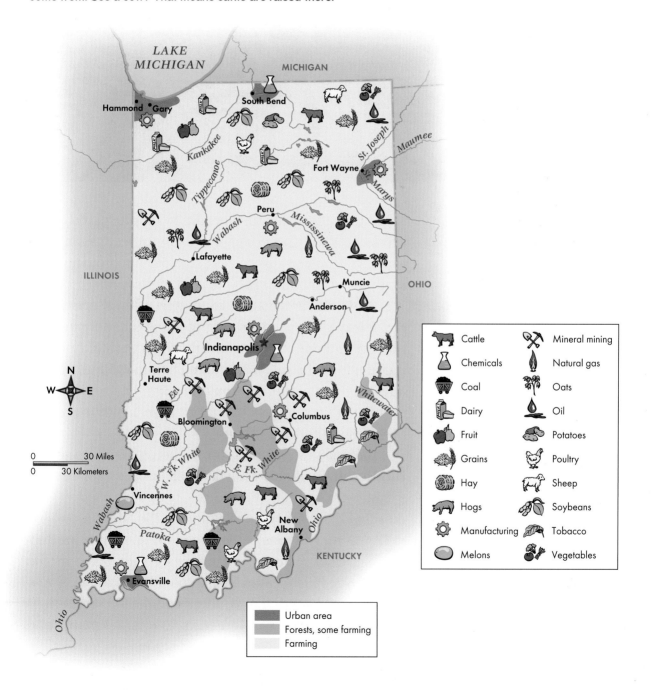

Cattle		Mineral mining	
Chemicals		Natural gas	
Coal		Oats	
Dairy		Oil	
Fruit		Potatoes	
Grains		Poultry	
Hay		Sheep	
Hogs		Soybeans	
Manufacturing		Tobacco	
Melons		Vegetables	

Urban area
Forests, some farming
Farming

A dairy cow on a milking machine in Zionsville

WORDS TO KNOW

biofuels *energy sources made from plants or plant-derived materials*

biodiesel *fuel made from soybeans and diesel oil*

Indiana is a leading producer of processed dairy products. Only California makes more ice cream than Indiana. Hoosier corn mills produce much of the corn syrup used in making soft drinks.

Biofuels are made from agricultural products. Some Indiana corn is used to produce ethanol, an alcohol that is blended with gasoline to make cleaner-burning fuel for cars. In 2013, Indiana had 13 ethanol plants. Together, the plants use roughly 431 million bushels of corn each year to produce more than 1 billion gallons (3.8 billion liters) of ethanol.

Indiana's soybean crop is being used to make **biodiesel**. Biodiesel can be used as a diesel fuel or mixed with regular diesel fuel. It can be used in any diesel vehicle. In Indiana, roughly 290 million pounds (132,000 metric tons) of soybean oil goes into producing biodiesel. The largest biodiesel fuel plant in the United States is located in Claypool, Indiana. It is able to produce more than 88 million gallons (333 million L) of biodiesel each year. Indiana's 13 ethanol plants and five biodiesel plants provide 620 jobs for Hoosier workers. The plants pump about $30 million into the local farm economy.

In 2011, miners took about 37 million tons of coal from Indiana's surface and underground deposits. The coal, however, contains a lot of sulfur and causes air pollution when it is burned. New technology for burning coal with less pollution allows some Indiana coal to be used as a fuel for electric power plants.

Indiana limestone is used in the construction industry. More than 230 million tons of limestone blocks are cut from Indiana quarries each year. About 25 million tons of sand and gravel are produced each year.

WOW

The National Cathedral in Washington, D.C., is built mainly of Indiana limestone, and it is one of the materials on the exterior of the Empire State Building in New York City.

HOOSIER-MADE GOODS

During the economic crisis of 2007–2009, many thousands of Hoosiers lost their jobs. Unemployment remains high, but the state economy is slowly improving, with manufacturing the strongest area of growth.

Indiana's number-one industry is making transportation equipment. Thousands of railroad cars, truck and bus bodies, motor homes, auto parts, and airplane parts roll off Hoosier assembly lines. Indiana also makes huge amounts of iron, steel, and chemicals. Indiana's chemical industry centers on drug manufacturing.

MINI-BIO

ELI LILLY: DRUG COMPANY FOUNDER

Eli Lilly (1838–1898) founded in Indianapolis what became one of the world's largest drug companies. Born in Maryland, Lilly moved with his family to Indiana. After serving as a Union army colonel during the Civil War, he set up a company in Indianapolis to make high-quality medicines that could be given only through doctors. Eventually, his son and grandsons took over the business. They built it into Eli Lilly & Company.

? **Want to know more?** Visit www.factsfornow .scholastic.com and enter the keyword **Indiana**.

FAQ ✦ ✦ ✦

Q8 WHAT IS THE BIGGEST COMPANY IN INDIANA?

A8 As of 2012, Berry Plastics Corporation of Evansville is Indiana's largest private company, with 15,000 employees in Indiana and elsewhere and revenues of nearly $4.8 billion.

MOTOR SPORTS INDUSTRY

Racing is more than just a sport in Indiana. Events at the Indianapolis Motor Speedway bring tourists as well as race teams to Indianapolis. From 2010 to 2012, three races—the Indianapolis 500, the Brickyard 400, and the United States Grand Prix—added an estimated $510 million each year to the economy of Indianapolis.

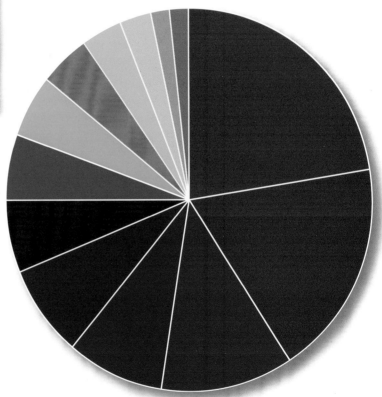

What Do Hoosiers Do?

This color-coded chart shows what industries Hoosiers work in.

22.5% Educational services, and health care and social assistance, 672,903

18.6% Manufacturing, 554,161

11.4% Retail trade, 338,891

8.8% Arts, entertainment, and recreation, and accommodation and food services, 262,256

7.7% Professional, scientific, and management, and administrative and waste management services, 228,859

6.1% Construction, 183,340

5.5% Finance and insurance, and real estate and rental and leasing, 164,022

5.3% Transportation and warehousing, and utilities, 157,358

4.6% Other services, except public administration, 138,515

3.5% Public administration, 105,098

2.8% Wholesale trade, 83,022

1.8% Information, 53,794

1.4% Agriculture, forestry, fishing and hunting, and mining, 42,283

Source: U.S. Census Bureau, 2010 census

HOOSIERS AT YOUR SERVICE

What do teachers, doctors, hairstylists, and pizza delivery people have in common? They are all service industry workers. Like many other states, the service industry plays a big role in Indiana's economy. Wholesale and retail sales are the top service industries. The service industry is the fastest-growing part of Indiana's economy. During the 1990s, service industry jobs grew by 40 percent. About 25 percent of all Hoosier workers hold jobs in the service industry.

Hoosiers are also looking to become leaders in new industries. One such industry is called logistics. Workers in the logistics industry use computers and other high-tech equipment to schedule shipments. They help transport goods from manufacturers to consumers quickly and at the lowest cost. Joanne Joyce, president and chief executive of the Indianapolis Private Industry Council, believes in helping young people acquire the skills they need to do these new jobs. "Central Indiana is the crossroads of America," she says, "and . . . we are ready to forge ahead as the crossroads of innovation and information."

This jewelry salesclerk is one of the many service workers in Indiana.

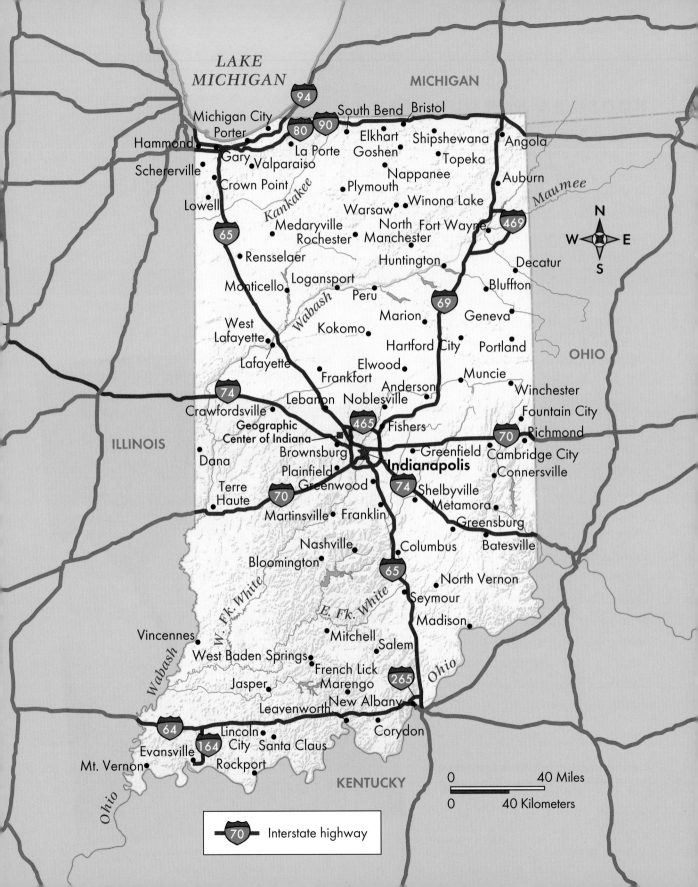

TRAVEL GUIDE TRAVEL GUIDE

CHAPTER NINE

TRAVEL GUIDE

TRAVEL GUIDE

★

FROM THE STUNNING SHORES OF LAKE MICHIGAN TO THE CAVES AND ROCK FORMATIONS NEAR THE OHIO RIVER, INDIANA IS A LAND OF STUNNING NATURAL BEAUTY. On a trip through Indiana, you can visit the state's fields and plains, hike its trails, observe its wildlife, and walk in the footsteps of people who lived long ago.

← Follow along with this travel map. We'll begin in Auburn and travel all the way to Vincennes.

NORTHERN

THINGS TO DO: Check out antique cars, shop for quilts, and scramble up a sand dune.

Auburn

★ **Auburn Cord Duesenberg Automobile Museum:** You'll see many fine automobiles produced in Indiana in the early 1900s and discover how the Indiana auto industry evolved from horse-drawn carriages to horseless carriages to full-scale automobile production.

Auburn Cord Duesenberg Automobile Museum

Bristol

★ **Bonneyville Mill:** Watch big belts moving and hear wheels creaking as water from the millpond turns the machinery that operates this 150-year-old gristmill. Bags of flour and cornmeal are for sale in the miller's shop.

Elkhart

★ **National New York Central Railroad Museum:** At this museum, you can learn about some of the railroad history that helped make Indiana the "Crossroads of America." Indoor and outdoor exhibits include videos, interactive displays, model railroads, and actual locomotives and railcars.

LaPorte

★ **LaPorte County Fair:** Indiana's oldest county fair is held every July at the LaPorte County Fairgrounds. You can view prize-winning animals, watch a horse race, and enjoy rides and other attractions at this authentic Hoosier experience.

Goshen

★ **Michiana Mennonite Relief Sale:** The centerpiece of this event, held at the Elkhart County Fairgrounds each September, is the Amish quilt auction. Start the day with a breakfast of pancakes and sausage, and stop by the antique auction and displays of crafts made all over the world.

★ **Hesston Steam Museum:** If it took a steam engine to run it, you will probably find it here. This outdoor museum of machines contains steam-driven devices of all kinds, including a locomotive, a sawmill, a steam crane, and a power plant. Taking a ride on a miniature train hauled by a miniature locomotive is fun for kids of all ages.

Medaryville

★ **Jasper-Pulaski State Fish & Wildlife Area:** Every autumn, this wildlife area fills with more than 10,000 greater sandhill cranes. The cranes stop off there on the way from their summer homes in Canada and northern states to Florida.

Michigan City

★ **Washington Park Zoo:** This cozy little zoo is located near the southern shore of Lake Michigan. The zoo's 250 animals are exhibited in natural settings. The Australian Avian Adventure exhibit allows visitors to enter a large aviary and feed parakeets and cockatiels.

Watching the tigers at Washington Park Zoo

Nappanee

★ **Amish Acres Historic Farm & Heritage Resort:** In a parklike setting, you can take a tour of an Amish farmhouse built in 1893, a round barn and other outbuildings, and a garden. Then ride a farm wagon around the grounds and see demonstrations of crafts such as quilting and candle making. At the Restaurant Barn, enjoy a family-style dinner with Amish favorites such as beef and noodles.

Peru

★ **Grissom Air Museum:** Visit this aviation museum and state historic site to see and touch warplanes that made history from World War II through the Gulf War. The museum is named in honor of astronaut Virgil "Gus" Grissom.

Indiana Dunes National Lakeshore

Porter

★ **Indiana Dunes National Lakeshore:** Learn all about dunes at the Calumet Dune Interpretive Center, hike miles of scenic trails, climb a dune, watch birds, or take a swim in Lake Michigan.

★ **Splash Down Dunes Water Park:** If swimming in Lake Michigan at the Indiana Dunes isn't exciting enough for you, travel inland and experience the attractions at this water park.

Shipshewana

★ **Menno-Hof Amish/Mennonite Information Center:** Learn about the Amish and Mennonite groups that live in this area of Indiana. You may enjoy looking at crafts in the town's shops and trying hearty Amish foods at the bakeries and restaurants.

South Bend

★ **South Bend Chocolate Factory and Museum:** Who doesn't like creamy chocolate candy? See how these treats are made and learn about the history of chocolate on a tour of this candy factory. Then finish off your visit with some free candy samples.

★ **Studebaker National Museum:** Learn about the history of Hoosier automobiles made from 1904 to 1966. Not only does the museum contain examples of Studebaker models, it also displays other fine cars once made in Indiana, as well as some horse-drawn carriages, including one used by President Abraham Lincoln.

Topeka

★ **Hoosier Buggy Shop:** Who makes horse-drawn carriages and buggies these days? The answer is the Hochstetler brothers in their Hoosier Buggy Shop. Take a tour to see how they are made.

Studebaker National Museum

Visitors at the Taltree Arboretum & Gardens

Valparaiso

★ **Taltree Arboretum & Gardens:** This retreat from urban life includes gardens, wetlands, woodlands, and prairies containing many varieties of prairie wildflowers, as well as thousands of oak and hickory trees.

Winona Lake

★ **The Village at Winona:** You can attend concerts and festivals and shop for artwork in this restored village along the shore of Winona Lake. The area was developed in the early 1900s as a summer retreat and conference grounds for several religious groups. You can tour the home of evangelist Billy Sunday, mentioned in the song "Chicago."

A visitor and sea lion at the Fort Wayne Children's Zoo

Fort Wayne

★ **Fort Wayne Children's Zoo:** Find penguins, monkeys, sea lions, and other creatures at this acclaimed children's zoo. See kangaroos, echidnas, sharks, and rays at Australian Adventure. Take a walk through the Indonesian Rainforest and pay a visit to the Komodo dragon. There are also pony rides, a dugout canoe ride, the Sky Safari, the Zoo Train, and an endangered species carousel.

★ **Foellinger-Freimann Botanical Conservatory:** These gardens are right in downtown Fort Wayne. The botanical conservatory has three indoor gardens and four outdoor gardens containing some 1,200 plants. The indoor Showcase Garden displays change with the seasons.

Monticello

★ **Indiana Beach Amusement Resort:** Hang on as you ride on five roller coasters and enjoy more than 20 other rides and attractions. The amusement park also contains a water park and swimming beach on Lake Shafer. You can even relax with a ride on the *Shafer Queen*, a paddle-wheel riverboat.

Indiana Beach Amusement Resort

CENTRAL

THINGS TO DO: Relive auto racing thrills, step back in time to a pioneer town, and admire great Native American art.

Cambridge City

★ **Huddleston Farmhouse:** See this spot where pioneers traveling the National Road to new homes in the West stopped to rest. Tour the buildings on the grounds to learn about the lives of pioneers traveling through the area.

Making pottery at the Conner Prairie Living History Museum Interactive History Park

Fishers

★ **Conner Prairie Interactive History Park:** Costumed guides take you on a tour of historic areas on this site near Indianapolis. You can see how French fur traders and Native Americans lived, visit a Victorian farmhouse, explore a pioneer village, and much more.

Geneva

★ **Limberlost:** This home in Adams County belonged to nature photographer and writer Gene (Geneva) Stratton-Porter. The area was once a swampland called Limberlost.

Dana

★ **Ernie Pyle WWII Museum:** The farmhouse where World War II correspondent Ernie Pyle was born is now

MINI-BIO 109

ERNIE PYLE: COURAGEOUS CORRESPONDENT

Reporter Ernest Taylor Pyle (1900–1945) was born on a farm near Dana. He traveled with U.S. troops during World War II to battlefields in Africa, Europe, and the South Pacific. People back home eagerly read his accounts of how the soldiers lived and fought. Pyle was killed by Japanese gunfire during the Battle of Okinawa.

? Want to know more? Visit www.factsfornow .scholastic.com and enter the keyword **Indiana**.

a museum. Exhibits tell about his career and his role in reporting from battlefields during World War II.

Indianapolis

★ **Eiteljorg Museum of American Indians and Western Art:** This is the only museum in the Midwest showing both Native American and American Western artwork. It contains works by traditional and contemporary artists, including N. C. Wyeth, Andy Warhol, Georgia O'Keeffe, Frederic Remington, and Kay WalkingStick.

★ **Benjamin Harrison Presidential Site:** The home where President Harrison once lived is now a library and museum. You can walk through 10 of the rooms in the large house and see how they were furnished when Harrison lived here.

★ **Indiana Historical Society:** The historical society contains a vast amount of information about Indiana's history and people. The collections include 50,000 digital images, 5,000 manuscript collections, 14,000 pieces of sheet music, and 1.6 million photographs. This is a great place to find primary sources.

★ **Indianapolis Motor Speedway Hall of Fame Museum:** This museum contains a collection of antique and racing cars, including more than 30 of the cars that have won the Indy 500. In a theater at the museum, you can watch a film about this classic auto race held almost every Memorial Day since 1911. The race was not held during the years of World War I or World War II.

SEE IT HERE!

CHILDREN'S MUSEUM OF INDIANAPOLIS
Hands-on exhibits bring learning to life. The "All Aboard..." exhibit celebrates the history of Indiana's railroads. Dinosphere takes visitors back 65 million years. Passport to the World introduces kids to other lands and cultures. In addition, there are changing events and activities throughout the year.

Metamora

★ **Whitewater Canal State Historic Site:** Take a 25-minute cruise on the *Ben Franklin III*, a canal boat pulled by a horse. Your ride is along one of the few Indiana canals that were built before the coming of the railroads.

FAQ

Q3 HAVE WOMEN EVER COMPETED IN THE INDY 500?

A3 Yes, nine women drivers competed in the race between 1977 and 2013. The first woman racer was Janet Guthrie.

Marion

★ **Quilters Hall of Fame:**
Established in the home of quilter
Marie Webster, the Hall of Fame
hosts changing exhibits of hand-
made quilts, representing a variety
of themes, throughout the year.

Fountain City

★ **Levi Coffin Home:** Imagine the
danger of escaping from slavery
using wagons with false bottoms
and safe houses with hidden doors.
You can see all this and more at
the redbrick home of Levi Coffin
and his wife, Catharine. It was one
of the stops on the Underground
Railroad.

Touring the Levi Coffin Home

Horseback riding at Brown County State Park

Nashville

★ **Brown County State Park:**
Covering 16,000 acres (6,500 ha),
this is Indiana's largest state park.
About 1.5 million visitors come
each year for pleasures such as a
self-guided walking tour around
the park's Ogle Hollow Nature
Preserve. There are 70 miles (113
km) of horseback riding trails and
12 miles (19 km) of steep, rugged
hiking trails.

★ **T. C. Steele State Historic Site:**
Tour the home where Hoosier
School painter Theodore Clement
Steele created his art in the early
1900s. In the studio, you can see
exhibits of his work. He often
painted scenes around this Brown
County summer home, which he
called "the House of the Singing
Winds."

SEE IT HERE!

A REAL COVER-UP

Beginning on the second Friday of October, Parke County celebrates its annual Covered Bridge Festival. Indiana has more than 90 covered bridges, and 31 of them are in Parke County. That is why the county calls itself the Covered Bridge Capital of the World. During the festival, you can hop aboard a bus at the courthouse in Rockville for tours that take you to some of the picture-perfect bridges.

Crawfordsville

★ **Turkey Run State Park:** Some of southern Indiana's most beautiful scenery lies inside the borders of this state park near Crawfordsville and along Sugar Creek. You can hike or horseback ride along the park's miles of trails that go through ancient forest. You can also rent a cabin on the grounds and stay the night.

Kayakers at Turkey Run State Park

SOUTHERN

THINGS TO DO: Hike rugged trails, wander through spectacular caves, or take a ride on an old-fashioned train.

Corydon

★ **Battle of Corydon Memorial Park:** This 5-acre (2 ha) state park was the site of Indiana's only Civil War battle. It is where the Harrison County Home Guard tried but failed to stop General John Hunt Morgan's Confederate troops after they crossed the Ohio River from Kentucky into Indiana. You can follow the route taken by Morgan from Corydon along the John Hunt Morgan Heritage Trail.

★ **Corydon State Capitol:** Indiana's first capitol was this square, limestone building built in the early 1800s. Hoosier lawmakers met here from 1816 to 1825. Exhibits inside tell about Indiana's early history.

French Lick-West Baden Springs

★ **Indiana Railway Museum:** See steam, electric, and diesel locomotives at this museum dedicated to Hoosier railroad history. The museum also has a large collection of antique passenger cars, freight cars, and cabooses. The highlight of a visit, however, is a two-hour ride aboard an old train along parts of the Hoosier National Forest and through a 2,200-foot (670 m) tunnel.

★ **West Baden Springs Hotel:** The mineral springs in this area have been popular since the late 1770s, when George Rogers Clark is said to have discovered them. Many people claimed that the mineral waters cured them of all kinds of diseases. They came to stay at hotels like the West Baden Springs Hotel. The historic hotel was restored and reopened in the early 2000s.

Jasper

★ **Dubois County Museum:** One of the largest county museums in Indiana is dedicated to the German immigrants who settled the area in the 1800s. Among the many exhibits are a log cabin and a ship's bunk like the ones immigrants squeezed into on the trip across the Atlantic Ocean.

Leavenworth

★ **Wyandotte Caves:** Take a guided tour through these beautiful limestone caves under the Harrison-Crawford State Forest. You will learn about the geology of Indiana that gave rise to huge underground rooms and fantastic rock formations.

Exploring Wyandotte Caves

Lincoln Boyhood National Memorial

Lincoln City

★ **Lincoln Boyhood National Memorial:** Walk the land where Abraham Lincoln spent his boyhood years from ages seven to 21. The site contains memorials to Lincoln and to his mother, Nancy, who is buried there. A museum tells about the boyhood life of Lincoln.

Madison

★ **Lanier Mansion State Historic Site:** This mansion was once the home of James Franklin Doughty Lanier, who helped bring railroads into Indiana. You can tour the house, stroll in the gardens, and learn about Lanier's contributions to the growth of Indiana.

Marengo

★ **Marengo Cave National Landmark:** See giant **stalactites** hanging from the ceiling of this spectacular cave, the only national landmark among the many caves in southern Indiana. You can admire an underground waterfall, walk through a "room" of lovely mineral crystals, and even pan for gemstones.

WORD TO KNOW

stalactites *columns or pillars formed on the ceiling of a cave from dripping groundwater*

Mitchell

★ **Spring Mill State Park:** History, hiking, and a whole lot more await visitors to this Indiana state park. You will find underground adventure in the park's Twin Caves, history at the Pioneer Village and Gristmill, and wildlife facts at the Nature Center.

Grinding corn at Spring Mill State Park

New Albany

★ **Culbertson Mansion:** Find out how the rich lived way back when. One of Indiana's wealthiest businessmen, William S. Culbertson, built this 25-room mansion in 1867. The mansion features hand-painted ceilings, marble fireplaces, and a carved rosewood staircase.

SEE IT HERE!

SKI SOUTHERN INDIANA?

Whether or not there is snow, Hoosiers can gather at Paoli Peaks for winter fun. Snowmaking equipment pumps the white flakes onto the 300-foot-high (90 m) natural hill. The slopes can hold more than 11,000 skiers or snowboarders per hour.

Rockport

★ **Lincoln Pioneer Village and Museum:** Set in a grassy park are log cabins, log houses, schools, churches, and other buildings that look just as they did when Abe Lincoln lived in Spencer County. Visit the museum to see items used in everyday life on the Hoosier frontier.

Santa Claus

★ **Holiday World & Splashin' Safari:** Yes, there is a Santa Claus, Indiana. It is home to a 100-acre (40 ha) theme park that features thrill rides, kids' rides, live shows, and a water park. Where did the town name come from? According to local legend, the German founders meeting at a church were searching for a suitable town name on Christmas Eve 1852. The wind blew the church doors open, and the people heard sleigh bells ringing outside. The children cried, "It's Santa Claus!"

Vincennes

★ **Vincennes State Historic Sites:** To get a feel for what life was like in old Vincennes, head for Harrison Street and the historic buildings preserved or reproduced there. Start with an orientation at the Log Cabin Visitors Center. Next door is the "Red House," the name lawmakers of Indiana Territory gave to their meeting place when Vincennes was the territorial capital. Then stop by the replica of the Elihu Stout Print Shop, where the laws of the territory, as well as its first newspaper, were printed.

WRITING PROJECTS

Check out these ideas for creating campaign brochures and researching famous Indianans. Or write you-are-there editorials.

118

ART PROJECTS

Create a great PowerPoint presentation, illustrate the state song, or learn about the state quarter and design your own.

119

TIMELINE

What happened when? This timeline highlights important events in the state's history—and shows what was happening throughout the United States at the same time.

122

FAST FACTS

Use this section to find fascinating facts about state symbols, land area and population statistics, weather, sports teams, and much more.

126

GLOSSARY

Remember the Words to Know from the chapters in this book? They're all collected here.

125

SCIENCE, TECHNOLOGY, ENGINEERING, & MATH PROJECTS

Make weather maps, graph population statistics, and research endangered species that live in the state.

120

PRIMARY VS. SECONDARY SOURCES

121

So what are primary and secondary sources? And what's the diff? This section explains all that and where you can find them.

BIOGRAPHICAL DICTIONARY

133

This at-a-glance guide highlights some of the state's most important and influential people. Visit this section and read about their contributions to the state, the country, and the world.

RESOURCES

Books and much more. Take a look at these additional sources for information about the state.

138

WRITING PROJECTS

Write a Memoir, Journal, or Editorial for Your School Newspaper!

Picture Yourself . . .

★ in a Mississippian home. What types of skills would you be learning? What would your responsibilities be? What kinds of crops would you be growing? How would life be different from the way your life is today?

SEE: Chapter Two, pages 29–30.

★ at Fort Ouiatenon. What types of people would you see there? What would people be doing, and why would they be bustling around?

SEE: Chapter Three, pages 36–37.

Create an Election Brochure or Web Site!

Run for office! Throughout this book, you've read about some of the issues that concern Indiana today. As a candidate for governor of Indiana, create a campaign brochure or Web site.

★ Explain how you meet the qualifications to be governor of Indiana.

★ Talk about the three or four major issues you'll focus on if you're elected.

★ Remember, you'll be responsible for Indiana's budget. How would you spend the taxpayers' money?

SEE: Chapter Seven, pages 84–85.

Create an interview script with a Hoosier!

★ Research various Hoosiers, such as Larry Bird, John G. Roberts Jr., Richard G. Hatcher, Madame C. J. Walker, Oscar Robertson, or Jane Pauley.

★ Based on your research, pick one person you would most like to talk with.

★ Write a script of the interview. What questions would you ask? How would this person answer? Create a question-and-answer format. You may want to supplement this writing project with a voice-recording dramatization of the interview.

SEE: Chapters Five, Six, and Seven, pages 56–91, and the Biographical Dictionary, pages 133–136.

ART PROJECTS

Create a PowerPoint Presentation or Visitors' Guide

Welcome to Indiana!

Indiana is a great place to visit and to live! From its natural beauty to its bustling cities and historical sites, there's plenty to see and do. In your PowerPoint presentation or brochure, highlight 10 to 15 of Indiana's amazing landmarks. Be sure to include:

★ a map of the state showing where these sites are located

★ photos, illustrations, Web links, natural history facts, geographic stats, climate and weather, plants and wildlife, and recent discoveries

SEE: Chapters One and Nine, pages 8–23 and 102–115, and Fast Facts, pages 126–127.

Illustrate the Lyrics to the Indiana State Song

("On the Banks of the Wabash, Far Away")

Use markers, paints, photos, collages, colored pencils, or computer graphics to illustrate the lyrics to "On the Banks of the Wabash, Far Away." Turn your illustrations into a picture book, or scan them into PowerPoint and add music.

SEE: The lyrics to "On the Banks of the Wabash, Far Away" on page 128.

State Quarter Project

From 1999 to 2008, the U.S. Mint introduced new quarters commemorating each of the 50 states in the order that they were admitted to the Union. Each state's quarter features a unique design on its back, or reverse.

GO TO: www.factsfornow.scholastic.com. Enter the keyword **Indiana** and look for the link to the Indiana quarter.

★ Research the significance of the image. Who designed the quarter? Who chose the final design?

★ Design your own Indiana quarter. What images would you choose for the reverse?

★ Make a poster showing the Indiana quarter and label each image.

SCIENCE, TECHNOLOGY, ENGINEERING, & MATH PROJECTS

Graph Population Statistics!

★ Compare population statistics (such as ethnic background, birth, death, and literacy rates) in Indiana counties or major cities.

★ In your graph or chart, look at population density and write sentences describing what the population statistics show; graph one set of population statistics and write a paragraph explaining what the graphs reveal.

SEE: Chapter Six, pages 66–79.

Create a Weather Map of Indiana!

Use your knowledge of Indiana's geography to research and identify conditions that result in specific weather events. What is it about the geography of Indiana that makes it vulnerable to things such as tornadoes? Create a weather map or poster that shows the weather patterns across the state. To accompany your map, explain the technology used to measure weather phenomena and provide data.

SEE: Chapter One, pages 8–23.

Karner blue butterfly

Track Endangered Species

Using your knowledge of Indiana's wildlife, research what animals and plants are endangered or threatened.

★ Find out what the state is doing to protect these species.

★ Chart known populations of the animals and plants, and report on changes in certain geographic areas.

SEE: Chapter One, pages 16–23.

PRIMARY VS. SECONDARY SOURCES

What's the Diff?

Your teacher may require at least one or two primary sources and one or two secondary sources for your assignment. So, what's the difference between the two?

★ **Primary sources are original.** You are reading the actual words of someone's diary, journal, letter, autobiography, or interview. Primary sources can also be photographs, maps, prints, cartoons, news/film footage, posters, first-person newspaper articles, drawings, musical scores, and recordings. By the way, when you conduct a survey, interview someone, shoot a video, or take photographs to include in a project, you are creating primary sources!

★ **Secondary sources are what you find in encyclopedias, textbooks, articles, biographies, and almanacs.** These are written by a person or group of people who tell about something that happened to someone else. Secondary sources also recount what another person said or did. This book is an example of a secondary source.

Now that you know what primary sources are—where can you find them?

★ **Your school or local library:** Check the library catalog for collections of original writings, government documents, musical scores, and so on. Some of this material may be stored on microfilm.

★ **Historical societies:** These organizations keep historical documents, photographs, and other materials. Staff members can help you find what you are looking for. History museums are also great places to see primary sources firsthand.

★ **The Internet:** There are lots of sites that have primary sources you can download and use in a project or assignment.

TIMELINE

★ ★ ★

U.S. Events | BCE | **Indiana Events**

c. 10,000 BCE
The first people arrive in Indiana.

1400

1450 CE
Mississippian people
abandon their city
at Angel Mounds.

1492
Christopher Columbus and his crew
sight land in the Caribbean Sea.

1600

1607
The first permanent English settlement in
North America is established at Jamestown.

1620
Pilgrims found Plymouth Colony, the
second permanent English settlement.

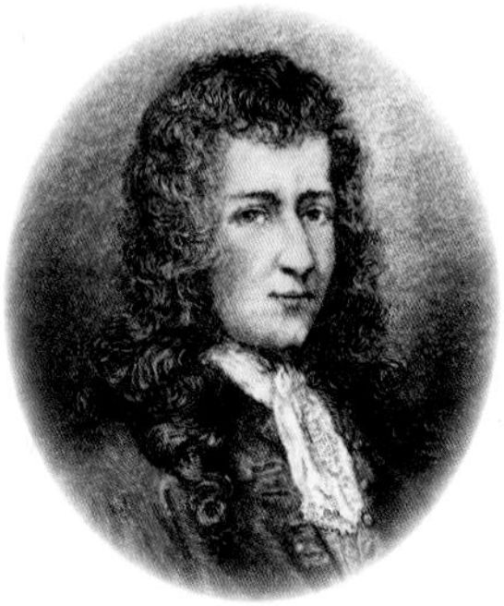

René Robert Cavelier,
Sieur de La Salle

1679
René-Robert Cavelier,
Sieur de La Salle, explores northern
Indiana, claiming it for France.

1700

1732
The French found Vincennes, Indiana's
first permanent European settlement.

1763
The British take over New France at the
end of the French and Indian War.

1776
Thirteen American colonies declare their
independence from Great Britain.

1779
George Rogers Clark recaptures
Fort Sackville from British forces.

1783
The United States wins British land that
becomes the Northwest Territory.

1787
The U.S. Constitution is written.

1795
The Treaty of Greenville gives lands in the
Northwest Territory to Native Americans.

U.S. Events | 1800 | Indiana Events

1800
Indiana Territory is created.

Tecumseh

1803
The Louisiana Purchase almost doubles the size of the United States.

1812–15
The United States and Great Britain fight the War of 1812.

1812
War of 1812 leads to Tecumseh being killed during a battle and many Native Americans agreeing to leave Indiana.

1813
Corydon becomes the capital of Indiana Territory.

1816
Indiana becomes the 19th state.

1825
Indianapolis becomes the state capital.

1830
The Indian Removal Act forces eastern Native American groups to relocate west of the Mississippi River.

1847
Indiana's first railroad is built.

1851
Indiana adopts its second constitution.

1861–65
The American Civil War is fought between the Northern Union and the Southern Confederacy; it ends with the surrender of the Confederate army, led by General Robert E. Lee.

1861–65
Indiana fights for the Union in the Civil War.

1863
President Abraham Lincoln frees all slaves in the Southern Confederacy with the Emancipation Proclamation.

1889
Standard Oil decides to build a refinery in Whiting.

1900

1904
The Studebaker Manufacturing Company of South Bend produces its first gasoline-powered car.

1917–18
The United States engages in World War I.

U.S. Events

Indiana Events

1908
The U.S. Steel Corporation
opens a mill in Gary.

1911
The first Indianapolis 500 race is held.

1929
The stock market crashes, plunging
the United States more deeply
into the Great Depression.

1933
About 25 percent of Hoosier workers are
unemployed during the Great Depression.

1941–45
The United States engages in World War II.

1941–45
Indiana industries produce weapons
and vehicles for use in World War II.

1950–53
The United States engages
in the Korean War.

1964–73
The United States engages
in the Vietnam War.

1967
Richard G. Hatcher is elected the
first black mayor of Gary.

1990s
Indiana's Hispanic
population grows
117 percent.

1991
The United States and other nations engage
in the brief Persian Gulf War against Iraq.

2000

2001
Terrorists hijack four U.S. aircraft and crash
them into the World Trade Center in New
York City, the Pentagon in Arlington, Virginia,
and a Pennsylvania field, killing thousands.

Chief Justice John G.
Roberts Jr.

2003
The Indiana Commission on
Hispanic/Latino Affairs is created.

2005
Indiana native John G. Roberts Jr. becomes
chief justice of the U.S. Supreme Court.

2012
Toyota announces it will expand its
manufacturing facility in Princeton.

GLOSSARY

★ ★ ★

abolitionists people who work to end slavery

allies people who are on the same side in a conflict

appeal a legal proceeding in which a court is asked to change the decision of a lower court

archaeologists people who study the remains of past human societies

biodiesel fuel made from soybeans and diesel oil

biofuels energy sources made from plants or plant-derived materials

choreographers people who design the steps for a dance performance

civil involving a dispute between individuals

civil rights basic human rights that all citizens in a society are entitled to, such as the right to vote

confederation an association of groups that comes together with common goals

excavated removed soil and rock from an area to dig up buried items

frugal careful with money

interurbans small trains or trolley cars connecting two or more cities

petitions written calls for action, usually with signatures of people who support the action

probate court a court that deals with wills and the property of people who have died

Prohibition a legal ban on the making or sale of liquor

receded pulled or moved back over time

secede to withdraw from a group or an organization

sponsor act as a person who proposes or creates a bill

stalactites columns or pillars formed on the ceiling of a cave from dripping groundwater

stocks monetary investments in a company

strike an organized refusal to work, usually as a sign of protest about working conditions

tributary a smaller river that flows into a larger river

union an organization formed by workers to try to improve working conditions and wages

urban sprawl the spread of a city and its suburbs into rural areas

FAST FACTS

★ ★ ★

State Symbols

Statehood date	December 11, 1816, the 19th state
Origin of state name	Latin for "land of the Indians"
State capital	Indianapolis
State nickname	Hoosier State
State motto	"The Crossroads of America"
State bird	Cardinal
State flower	Peony
State tree	Tulip poplar (yellow poplar)
State stone	Limestone
State song	"On the Banks of the Wabash, Far Away"
State fair	Mid-August at Indianapolis

State seal

Geography

Total area; rank	36,418 square miles (94,322 sq km); 38th
Land; rank	35,867 square miles (92,895 sq km); 38th
Water; rank	551 square miles (1,427 sq km); 39th
Inland water; rank	316 square miles (818 sq km); 43rd
Great Lakes; rank	235 square miles (609 sq km); 8th
Geographic center	Boone County, 14 miles (23 km) north-northwest of Indianapolis
Latitude	37° 47' N to 41° 46' N
Longitude	84° 49' W to 88° 4' W
Highest point	Hoosier Hill, 1,257 feet (383 m), in Wayne County
Lowest point	Along the Ohio River, 320 feet (98 m)
Largest city	Indianapolis
Number of counties	92
Longest river	Wabash, 475 miles (764 km)

Population

Population; rank (2010 census)	6,483,802; 15th
Density (2010 census)	181 persons per square mile (68 per sq km)
Population distribution (2010 census)	72.4% urban, 27.6% rural
Ethnic distribution (2010 census)	White persons: 81.5%
	Black persons: 9.0%
	Asian persons: 1.6%
	American Indian and Alaska Native persons: 0.2%
	People of two or more races: 1.5%
	Hispanic or Latino persons: 6.0%
	People of some other race: 0.1%

Weather

Record high temperature	116°F (47°C) at Collegeville on July 14, 1936
Record low temperature	−36°F (−38°C) at New Whiteland on January 19, 1994
Average July temperature, Indianapolis	74°F (23°C)
Average January temperature, Indianapolis	26°F (−3°C)
Average annual precipitation, Indianapolis	40 inches (102 cm)

State flag

STATE SONG

"On the Banks of the Wabash, Far Away"

Words and music by Paul Dresser
The state legislature adopted this as the official song in 1913.

'Round my Indiana homestead wave the cornfields,
In the distance loom the woodlands clear and cool.
Oftentimes my thoughts revert to scenes of childhood,
Where I first received my lessons, nature's school.
But one thing there is missing in the picture,
Without her face it seems so incomplete,
I long to see my mother in the doorway,
As she stood there years ago, her boy to greet.

Chorus:
Oh, the moonlight's fair tonight along the Wabash,
From the fields there comes the breath of new-mown hay,
Through the sycamores the candle lights are gleaming,
On the banks of the Wabash, far away.

Many years have passed since I strolled by the river,
Arm in arm, with sweetheart Mary by my side,
It was there I tried to tell her that I loved her,
It was there I begged of her to be my bride.
Long years have passed since I strolled thro' the churchyard.
She's sleeping there, my angel, Mary dear,
I loved her, but she thought I didn't mean it,
Still I'd give my future were she only here.
(Chorus)

NAT**U**RAL AREAS AN**D**
HISTORIC SITES

★ ★ ★

National Memorial

Indiana's only national memorial is the *Lincoln Boyhood National Memorial*, which preserves the site where Abraham Lincoln lived between the ages of 7 and 21.

National Lakeshore

Indiana boasts a beautiful national lakeshore at the *Indiana Dunes National Lakeshore*. It is a great spot for hiking, swimming, biking, bird-watching, and wildlife viewing. Located on the southern shores of Lake Michigan, this lakeshore includes dunes, marshes, woodlands, a river, and a bog.

National Historical Park

The *George Rogers Clark National Historical Park* commemorates an event in 1779, in which frontiersmen led by Lieutenant Colonel George Rogers Clark captured the British fort formerly on this site, a charge that is still heralded as one of the great feats of the American Revolution.

National Forest

Hoosier National Forest in southern Indiana covers almost 200,000 acres (80,000 ha). It contains various smaller sites, including the Pioneer Mothers Memorial Forest, an old-growth forest; Hemlock Cliffs, which overlook a sandstone canyon; and Hickory Ridge Lookout Tower, which is listed on the National Historic Lookout Register.

State Parks and Forests

The Indiana State Park system maintains 24 state parks and recreation areas, including *Indiana Dunes State Park*, which features beautiful sand dune landscapes aside Lake Michigan; the *Falls of the Ohio State Park*, which features a fossil bedrock dating back millions of years; the *Spring Mill State Park*, which is home to a pioneer village with a historic gristmill; and *Whitewater Memorial State Park*, which was built as a World War II memorial.

SPORTS TEAMS

★　★　★

NCAA Teams (Division I)

Ball State University *Cardinals*
Butler University *Bulldogs*
Indiana State University *Sycamores*
Indiana University–Bloomington *Hoosiers*
Indiana University-Purdue University Fort Wayne *Mastodons*
Indiana University-Purdue University Indianapolis *Jaguars*
Purdue University *Boilermakers*
University of Evansville *Aces*
University of Notre Dame *Fighting Irish*
Valparaiso University *Crusaders*

PROFESSIONAL SPORTS TEAMS

★　★　★

National Basketball Association

Indiana *Pacers*

Women's National Basketball Association

Indiana *Fever*

National Football League

Indianapolis *Colts*

CULT RAL INSTITUTINS

★   ★   ★

Libraries

The *Indiana State Library* has information on the history of the state and its citizens, along with genealogical records for family history research.

The *Indiana University-Purdue University Indianapolis Library* includes a special philanthropic library, as well as government statistics, information on the state, and general collections.

Opened in the late 19th century, the *Willard Library* in Evansville is Indiana's oldest public library building. It includes the Thrall Art Book Collection and a rich supply of genealogical resources.

Museums

The *General Lew Wallace Study & Museum* (Crawfordsville) contains items collected by Wallace during his life as an author, soldier, statesman, artist, violinist, and inventor.

The *Great Lakes Museum of Military History* (Michigan City) contains rare documents, old military uniforms, medals, and weapons used in combat.

The *Indiana Railway Museum* (French Lick) gives train rides through parts of Hoosier National Forest, including one of the longest railroad tunnels in Indiana.

The *Indiana State Museum* (Indianapolis) contains a wealth of information on the state, such as radio and television broadcast history, sports history, and prehistoric exhibits.

The *Indianapolis Museum of Art* is one of the largest and oldest art museums in the country. Lush gardens surround the building.

Performing Arts

The *Indiana Ballet Theatre* (Merrillville, DeMotte) has presented dance performances to the people of northwest Indiana for more than 30 years. It also offers classes for aspiring dancers.

The *Indianapolis Symphony Orchestra* (Indianapolis) is the largest performing arts organization in Indiana. It has been performing since 1930.

Universities and Colleges

In 2011, Indiana had 15 public and 60 private institutions of higher learning.

ANNUAL EVENTS

January–March

Winter sports in LaPorte and New Carlisle (January and February)

Parke County Maple Syrup Fair in Rockville (February–March)

Indiana High School Athletic Association State Basketball Tournament in Indianapolis (March)

April–June

Mushroom Festival in Mansfield (April)

Sugar Creek Canoe Race in Crawfordsville (April)

Marion Easter Pageant (April or May)

Indianapolis 500 Race and Festival (Memorial Day weekend)

Bluegrass Music Festival in Beanblossom (June)

Glass Festival in Greentown (June)

Miss Indiana Pageant in Michigan City (June)

July–September

Freedom Festival in Evansville (June and July)

Circus City Festival in Peru (July)

Hydroplane Regatta in Madison (July)

Indiana State Fair in Indianapolis (August)

National Muzzle Loading Rifle Association Championship Shoot in Friendship (August)

Daviess County Turkey Trot Festival (September)

October–December

Harvest Homecoming in New Albany (October)

Parke County Covered Bridge Festival in Rockville (October)

Indianapolis Christmas Lighting Ceremony (November and December)

Traditional Christmas at the Conner Prairie Interactive History Park (November and December)

Indiana Day across the state (December 11)

BIOGRAPHICAL DICTIONARY

Albion Fellows Bacon (1865–1933) of Evansville was a writer and social reformer. The Albion Fellows Bacon Center to prevent domestic abuse was named in her honor.

David Nathaniel Baker (1931–) is an award-winning jazz musician, professor, and chair of the Jazz Department at Indiana University School of Music in Bloomington.

Anne Baxter (1923–1985) starred in films such as *All About Eve* and *The Ten Commandments*. She was born in Michigan City.

Evan Bayh (1955–) served as Indiana's governor from 1988 to 1997 and was elected to the U.S. Senate in 1999.

Joshua Bell (1967–) is an award-winning violinist. He was born in Bloomington.

Larry Bird See page 77.

Bill Blass (1922–2002), born in Fort Wayne, was an award-winning clothing designer. From 1976 to 1992, he also helped design Continental Mark cars for the Ford Motor Company.

Frank Borman (1928–), a native of Gary, served as an astronaut in the Apollo space program. With two other astronauts, he made the first flight around the moon.

Norman Bridwell (1928–) is a children's book author and illustrator who developed Clifford the Big Red Dog. He was born in Kokomo.

Norman Bridwell

Robert Lee Brokenburr (1886–1974), a lawyer, was the first African American elected to the Indiana state senate (served 1941–1944).

George Washington Buckner See page 86.

Dorothy Richard Buell See page 21.

Hoagland "Hoagy" Carmichael (1899–1981) composed popular songs from the 1920s through the 1950s, including hits such as "Stardust" and "In the Cool, Cool, Cool of the Evening." He was born in Bloomington.

Oscar Charleston (1896–1954) was a baseball player in the Negro Leagues. He was inducted into the Baseball Hall of Fame in 1976. Indianapolis was his hometown.

George Rogers Clark (1752–1818) was a lieutenant colonel in the Virginia militia during the American Revolution. He played a big part in winning the Northwest Territory for the United States.

Oscar Charleston

Levi Coffin See page 50.

Jim Davis (1945–), a native of Marion, draws the cartoon cat Garfield. He based his cartoon character on a grouchy cat that lived on his family farm.

James Dean (1931–1955), an actor, starred in the films *East of Eden* and *Rebel Without a Cause*. He was born in Marion.

Eugene V. Debs See page 52.

Theodore Dreiser (1871–1945), who was born in Terre Haute, was a writer. His first great novel was *Sister Carrie*.

Shirley Graham Du Bois (1896–1977) was an African American playwright and biographer of great African Americans such as Phillis Wheatley and Frederick Douglass. She was born in Evansville.

Jenna Fischer (1974–) is an American actress and director from Fort Wayne. She is best known for her role on the TV comedy *The Office*. She has also appeared in films, including *Walk Hard* and *Hall Pass*.

William Forsyth (1854–1935) was a painter in a movement called the Hoosier School. He founded an art school in Muncie and taught at the John Herron Art Institute in Indianapolis.

Vivica A. Fox (1964–) of South Bend is a popular motion picture and television actress.

Brendan Fraser (1968–) is a film actor who has appeared in the three-part Mummy film series, *Looney Tunes: Back in Action*, *Journey to the Center of the Earth*, *Inkheart*, and *Crash*. He was born in Indianapolis.

James Bert Garner (1870–1960) was a chemist and professor who invented a life-saving World War I gas mask in 1915.

Brendan Fraser

Crystal Gayle (1951–), born in Kentucky but raised in Indiana, is a country music star famous for the hit song "Don't It Make My Brown Eyes Blue."

William Auge "Will" Geer (1902–1978) was an actor who is best remembered for his role as the grandpa in the 1970s TV series *The Waltons*. He was born in Frankfort.

Ron Glass (1945–), who was born in Evansville, played roles in a number of television sitcoms. His most famous role was as Detective Ron Harris on *Barney Miller*, which aired in the 1970s and 1980s.

Virgil "Gus" Grissom (1926–1967), a native of Mitchell, was one of the original astronauts selected in 1959 for the U.S. space program and the second U.S. astronaut to fly in space.

Johnny Gruelle (1880–1938) was a cartoonist who designed the Raggedy Ann doll. He went on to create the Raggedy Ann and Andy series of children's books. He grew up in Indianapolis.

Virgil "Gus" Grissom

Charles "Buster" Hall (1920–1971) was the first African American aviator to shoot down a German warplane during World War II. He was from Brazil, Indiana.

Katie B. Hall (1938–2012) was the first African American woman from Indiana elected to the U.S. House of Representatives (1982–1985).

Benjamin Harrison See page 88.

William Henry Harrison See page 88.

Richard G. Hatcher See page 63.

Florence Henderson (1934–), who was born in Dale, is an actress and singer. She played Carol Brady in TV's *The Brady Bunch*, a successful sitcom that ran from 1969 to 1974.

Theodore M. Hesburgh (1917–) is a Roman Catholic priest, educator, and writer who was president of the University of Notre Dame from 1952 to 1987.

Felrath Hines (1913–1993) was an African American civil rights activist and artist. He was born in Indianapolis.

James Hoffa (1913–?), a native of Brazil, Indiana, was a controversial labor leader. He disappeared in 1975 and was never seen again. He was declared dead in 1982.

Robert Indiana (1928–), who was born Robert Clark in New Castle, is a sculptor who makes art out of letters and numbers.

Janet Jackson (1966–) is a pop music star and member of the Jackson family of musicians that includes sister La Toya and included brother Michael. She is from Gary.

Michael Jackson (1958–2009), who was from Gary, first sang with his four older brothers in a group called the Jackson 5. In 1979, his first solo album, *Off the Wall*, became the first record to chart four top-10 hits.

Janet Jackson

Annie Fellows Johnston (1863–1931) was a children's book author who invented a young girl nicknamed the Little Colonel. Johnston grew up in McCutchanville.

Percy Julian See page 73.

Greg Kinnear (1963–) is a television talk show host and actor who has appeared in many films, including *As Good As It Gets* and *Little Miss Sunshine*. He was born in Logansport.

René-Robert Cavelier, Sieur de La Salle See page 35.

David Letterman (1947–), a native of Indianapolis, is a comedian and television talk show host. Since 1993, he has hosted the *Late Show with David Letterman*.

Eli Lilly See page 99.

Abraham Lincoln See page 88.

Carole Lombard (1908–1942), born Jane Alice Peters in Fort Wayne, was an actor in such films as *Mr. & Mrs. Smith* and *To Be or Not to Be*.

Shelley Long (1949–) is an actor and screenwriter best known for her role in the TV comedy *Cheers* during the 1980s. She is from Fort Wayne.

Richard Green Lugar (1932–) was a U.S. senator from Indiana from 1977 to 2013. Before being elected to the Senate, he was mayor of Indianapolis from 1968 to 1975.

Karl Malden (1912–2009) was a stage and screen actor whose movies include *On the Waterfront* and *A Streetcar Named Desire*, for which he won an Oscar. He grew up in Gary.

Jon McLaughlin (1982–) is a pop singer and songwriter from Anderson. His biggest hit is "Beating My Heart" from his second album, *OK Now*.

Steve McQueen (1930–1980), born in Beech Grove, was an actor of the 1960s and 1970s. One of his biggest hits was the film *Bullitt*.

John Mellencamp (1951–) is a rock singer and songwriter. Early in his career, he performed as John Cougar. He was born in Seymour.

John Mellencamp

Dale Messick (1906–2005), from South Bend, created a comic strip about a newspaper reporter named Brenda Starr.

Jane Pauley

Jane Pauley (1950–), a native of Indianapolis, cohosted NBC's *Today* show in the 1970s and 1980s. She then created the feature news program that became *Dateline*.

Bill Peet (1915–2002), born William Bartlett Peet in Grandview, was a screenwriter, cartoonist, and the author and illustrator of 35 children's books. He wrote the screenplay for *101 Dalmatians*.

Sydney Pollack (1934–2008), born in Lafayette, was a film director and producer. In 1986, he won Oscars for Best Picture and Best Director for *Out of Africa*.

Pontiac See page 38.

Cole Porter See page 74.

John Wesley Posey See page 70.

Ernie Pyle See page 109.

Orville Redenbacher (1907–1995) began selling his special popping corn in 1970, after experimenting with thousands of different types of popcorn. As advertising spokesman for his popcorn, he became a celebrity. He was born in Brazil, Indiana, and attended Purdue University in West Lafayette.

John G. Roberts Jr. See page 87.

Oscar Robertson See page 79.

Knute Rockne See page 59.

Colonel Harland David Sanders (1890–1980) was a businessman and founder of the Kentucky Fried Chicken restaurant chain. He was born in Henryville.

William M. Scholl (1882–1968), better known as "Dr. Scholl," developed foot-care products.

May Wright Sewall (1844–1920) worked to help women gain the right to vote. She also founded a school for girls in Indianapolis.

Zerna Addis Sharp (1889–1981) a native of Hillisburg was an author and teacher. She is famous for creating the Dick and Jane beginning-reader books that taught millions of children in the United States how to read.

Jean Shepherd (1921–1999) was a radio personality, short-story writer, and screenwriter who wrote the movie *A Christmas Story* based on his childhood in Hammond.

Red Skelton (1913–1997) was a popular radio and television comedian from Vincennes. From 1951 to 1971, he had his own TV show.

Theodore Clement Steele (1847–1926) was a painter who belonged to the Hoosier School. Admirers especially treasure his depiction of natural light in landscape paintings.

Tony Stewart (1971–) is a NASCAR-champion racing car driver and team owner. He was born in Columbus.

Tony Stewart

George P. Stewart (1874–1924) helped found the *Indianapolis Recorder* in the 1890s. This newspaper for African Americans is still published today.

Gene Stratton-Porter (1863–1924) was an author and photographer. Her novel *Freckles* is set in central Indiana. She was born in Wabash County.

Twyla Tharp

Booth Tarkington (1869–1946), a novelist, won the Pulitzer Prize for fiction in 1919 for *The Magnificent Ambersons* and in 1922 for *Alice Adams*. He was born in Indianapolis.

Twyla Tharp (1941–) is a dancer, director, and choreographer who has won Tony and Emmy awards. She was born in Portland.

Tara VanDerveer See page 78.

Kurt Vonnegut Jr. (1922–2007) wrote satirical novels, often with a science-fiction twist, including *Slaughterhouse Five*. He was from Indianapolis.

Madam C. J. Walker See page 55.

Lew Wallace (1827–1905) was a Union army colonel and lawyer who wrote *Ben-Hur*, a historical novel set in the time of the ancient Roman empire. He was born in Brookville.

Michael Warren (1946–) is an actor best known for his role as officer Bobby Hill in the 1980s TV crime series *Hill Street Blues*. He was born in South Bend.

Marie D. Webster (1859–1956) wrote *Quilts: Their Story and How to Make Them* (1915). She is a member of the Quilters Hall of Fame, and her home in Marion is its headquarters.

Jessamyn West (1902–1984) wrote stories about the Quakers in Indiana. Her best-known stories are *The Friendly Persuasion* and *Except for Me and Thee*.

Ryan White (1971–1990) was a Kokomo teenager and activist who worked to end discrimination against people with AIDS.

Robert Wise (1914–2005) was an Academy Award–winning producer and director of such films as *The Sound of Music* and *West Side Story*. He was born in Winchester.

Wilbur Wright (1867–1912), with his brother Orville, invented and flew the first airplane. Wilbur was born in Millville.

Frank "Fuzzy" Zoeller (1951–), born in New Albany, is a professional golfer who has won two major championships. He won the Masters Tournament in 1979 and the U.S. Open in 1984.

Michael Warren

RESOURCES

BOOKS

Nonfiction

Derzipilski, Kathleen. *Indiana*. New York: Marshall Cavendish Benchmark, 2012.

Kramer, Ralph. *The Indianapolis 500: A Century of Excitement*. Iola, Wis.: Krause Publications, 2010.

Laxer, James. *Tecumseh*. Toronto, Ontario, Canada: Groundwood Books, 2012.

Schoon, Kenneth J. *Dreams of Duneland: A Pictorial History of the Indiana Dunes Region*. Bloomington, Ind.: Indiana University Press, 2013.

Silverman, Steve. *The Story of the Indiana Pacers*. Mankato, Minn.: Creative Education, 2011.

Fiction

Homan, Lynn M., Thomas Reilly, and Rosalie Shepherd (illustrator). *The Tuskegee Airmen Story*. Gretna, La.: Pelican Publishing Company, 2002.

Johnston, Annie Fellows. *The Little Colonel*. Illustrated Edition. Bel Air, Calif.: Dodo Press, 2006.

Peet, Bill. *The Whingdingdilly*. Boston: Houghton Mifflin, 1982.

Riley, James Whitcomb. *Little Orphant Annie and Other Poems*. Mineola, N.Y.: Dover Publications, 1994.

Stratton-Porter, Gene. *Freckles*. Winnetka, Calif.: Norilana Books, 2006.

Thrasher, Crystal. *The Dark Didn't Catch Me*. Bloomington: Indiana University Press, 2004.

Visit this Scholastic Web site for more information on Indiana:
www.factsfornow.scholastic.com
Enter the keyword **Indiana**

INDEX

★ ★ ★

Page numbers in *italics* indicate illustrations.

abolitionists, 50, *50*, 70, *70*
Adena people, 28
African Americans, 36, 37, 46, 48, 50, 54–55, 58, 61, 62, 63, 64, 67, 69, 86, 133, 134
agriculture, *12*, 13, 18, 28, 29, 51, 57, 60–61, 70, *70*, 71, 96, *96*, 97, 98
Albion Fellows Bacon Center, 133
Algonquian people, 30, *30*, 44
Allen, Joseph P., 73
American Railway Union, 52
Amish Acres Historic Farm & Heritage Resort, 105
Amish people, 71, 75–76, *76*, 105, 106
Andretti, John, 79, *79*
Angel Mounds, 29, 30, 34
animal life, 17, 18, *18*, 20, *24*, 26, 28, 37, 60, 70, 96, 105, *105*, 108, *108*
Archaic people, 27
Armstrong, Louis, 59
art, 61, 76, 109, 111, 134
artifacts, 26, 27, *27*, *30*
astronauts, 73
Auburn, 59, 104, *104*
Auburn Cord Duesenberg Automobile Museum, 104, *104*
automobile manufacturing, 51, 52–53, 55, 64–65, 94, 95, 99, 104, *104*, 107
automobile racing, 53, *53*, 79, *79*, 100, 110, *110*

Bacon, Albion Fellows, 133
Baker, David Nathaniel, 133
Ball State University, 72, 74
baseball, 78, 133, *133*
basketball, *77*, *77*, 78, 79, *79*
Battle of Corydon Memorial Park, 112
Battle of Fallen Timbers, 45
Battle of the Thames, 45
Battle of Tippecanoe, *44*, 45, 88

Baxter, Anne, 133
Bayh, Evan, 133
Bell, Joshua, *75*, *75*, 133
Benjamin Harrison Presidential Site, 110
Berry Plastics Corporation, 100
biofuels, 98
Bird, Larry, *77*, *77*
Black, Glenn A., 30
"Black Law," 48
Black Orchid club, 59
Blass, Bill, 133
Bloomington, 72
Bonneyville Mill, 104
borders, 12
Borman, Frank, 73, 133
Bowersox, Ken, 73
Brickyard 400, 79, 100
Bridwell, Norman, 73, 133, *133*
Bristol, 104
British settlers, 37–38, 40, *40*
Brokenburr, Robert Lee, 63, 133
Brown County State Park, 111, *111*
Buckner, George Washington, 86, *86*
Buell, Dorothy Richard, 21, *21*, 23

Calumet Dune Interpretive Center, 106
Cambridge City, 108
canals, 110
canoes, 30, 35, 36, 37, 41
Carmichael, Hoagland "Hoagy," 133
caves, 9, 13, 113, *113*, 114
Charleston, Oscar, 133, *133*
Charlestown State Park, 27
Chase Tower, 64
Children's Museum of Indianapolis, 110
Civil War, 51, *51*, 88, 99
Clark, George Rogers, 38, 39–40, *39*, 41, 113, 133
Clarksville, 41
Claypool, 98
climate, 11, 14–15, *15*, 15–16, 26
Coffin, Catharine, 50, 111

Coffin, Levi, 50, *50*, 111
Colfax, Schuyler, 90
College Football Hall of Fame, 106, *106*
Collegeville, 16
Conner Prairie Interactive History Park, 109, *109*
construction industry, 99
Corydon, 48, 51, 82, 112
Corydon State Capitol, 112
counties, 88, *89*, 90
Courts in the Classroom, 87
Covered Bridge Festival, 112
crafts, 29, 75–76, 104, 105, 106
Crawfordsville, 112
Culbertson Mansion, 115
Culbertson, William S., 115

dairy farming, 98, *98*
Dale, 113
Dana, 109
dance, 75, 137, *137*
Davis, Jim, 73, 133
Dean, James, 74, 133
Debs, Eugene V., 52, *52*
Delaware people, 30
Douglas, Paul H., 23
Dreiser, Theodore, 133
Dr. Ted's Musical Marvels, 113
drug manufacturing, 99
drumlins, 13
Dubois County Museum, 113
Du Bois, Shirley Graham, 134

earthquakes, 11
East Chicago, 52, 55
Easton, Rufus, 46
education, 54, 72–73, *72*, 81, 84, 87, *88*, 91
Eiteljorg Museum of American Indians and Western Art, 109
elections, 84, 86–87
electricity, 57, 99
elevation, 9, *10*, 11
Elkhart, 104
England, Anthony W., 73
environmental protection, 18–20
Ernie Pyle WWII Museum, 109

Erskine, Carl, 78
ethnic groups, 54–55, 67, 68–69, *68*, 90
European exploration, 30, *32*, 33, *34, 35, 35*
European settlers, 33, 36, 37, 108
Evansville, 14, 29, 48, 69, 100
executive branch of government, 84, 85

Fairbanks, Charles W., 90
Fever basketball team, 78
Fischer, Jenna, 134
Fisher, Carl, 53
Fishers, 109
flooding, 15, 39, *39*
Foellinger-Freimann Botanical Conservatory, 108
foods, 27, 29, 70, *70*, 71, *71*, 96, 105, 106, *106*
football, 59, *77*, 78, *78, 106*
Ford, Kevin A., 73
forests, 11, 16, *17*, 26, 108, 112, *112*, 113
Forsyth, William, 134
Fort Detroit, 39
Fort Ouiatenon, 34, 36, 37
Fort Sackville, 34, 38, 39, *40, 41*
Fort Wayne, 44, 69, 74, 108
Fort Wayne Children's Zoo, 108, *108*
Fountain City, 111
Fox, Vivica A., 134
Fraser, Brendan, 134, *134*
French and Indian War, 37
French exploration, *32*, 33, 35, *35*
French Lick, 112–113
French settlers, 33, 36, 37, 109
Fugitive Slave Law, 50
fur trade, 33, 36–37, *36*, 109

Gambetta, Ricardo, 90
Garner, James Bert, 134
Gary, 52, 54, *54*, 55, 62, 63, *63*, 64, 69, 73, 74, *88*
Gary, Elbert, 52
Gayle, Crystal, 75, 134
Geer, William Auge "Will," 134
General Assembly, 86, 92
Geneva, 109
George Rogers Clark National Historical Park, 41
glaciers, 11, 13

Glass, Ron, 134
Goose Pond, 16
Gordon, Jeff, 79
Goshen, 104–105
Government Center, 83–84
Great Depression, 60–61
Great Lakes Plains region, 12–13
Grissom Air Museum, 106
Grissom, Virgil "Gus," 73, 134, *134*
gristmills, 104, 114, *114*
Gruelle, Johnny, 73, 134
Guthrie, Janet, 110

Hall, Charles "Buster," 61, 134
Hall, Katie B., 134
Hammond, 64, 73
Harmonists, 48
Harrison, Benjamin, 88, 110
Harrison County Home Guard, 51, 112
Harrison-Crawford State Forest, 113
Harrison, William Henry, 45, 48, 88
Hatcher, Richard G., 63, *63*
Henderson, Florence, 134
Hendricks, Thomas A., 90
Hesburgh, Theodore M., 134
Hesston Steam Museum, 105
Hines, Felrath, 135
Hispanics, 64, 67, 69, 90
Hoffa, James, 135
Holiday World & Splashin' Safari, 115
"home rule," 90
Hoosier Buggy Shop, 107
Hoosier Helper tow trucks, 70
Hoosier Hill, 9, 11
Hoosier National Forest, *17*, 113
"Hoosier" nickname, 51, 70
Hoosier School art movement, 76, 111, 134, 136
Hoosiers (movie), 77
Hopewell culture, 29
housing, 27, 29, *29*, 30, 62
Huddleston Farmhouse, 108

ice age, 11, 25, 26
immigrants, 54–55, 58, 68, 113
indentured servants, 48
Indiana Beach Amusement Resort, 108, *108*

Indiana Dunes National Lakeshore, *8*, 21, 23, *23*, 59, 106
Indiana Historical Society, 30, 110
Indianapolis, 18, 48, 49, 52, 54, *56*, 59, 62, 64, 65, 69, *80*, 82, *82, 83*, 90, 91, *91*, 109–110
Indianapolis 500 auto race, 53, *53*, 79, *79*, 100, 110, *110*
Indianapolis City Market, *65*
Indianapolis Colts football team, 78, *78*
Indianapolis Freeman newspaper, 55
Indianapolis Motor Speedway, 53, *53*, 79, 100, 110
Indianapolis Motor Speedway Hall of Fame Museum, 110
Indianapolis Private Industry Council, 101
Indianapolis Symphony Orchestra, 75
Indiana Railway Museum, 112–113
Indiana, Robert, 76, 135
Indiana Territory, *7*, 45, *47*, 48, 115
Indiana Toll Road, 70
Indiana University, 30, 72, *77*, 133
insect life, 17, 18, *18*
interstate highways, 49, 61, 81, *102*
interurban trains, 52
Iroquois people, 30

Jackson Five, 75
Jackson, Janet, 75, 135, *135*
Jackson, La Toya, 75
Jackson, Michael, 75, 135
Jasper, 113
Jasper-Pulaski State Fish & Wildlife Area, 105
jazz music, 59, 133
jobs, 19, 21, 54, 57, 58, 61, 62, 63, 64, *91*, 94, 99, *100*, 101
John Hunt Morgan Heritage Trail, 112
Johnston, Annie Fellows, 73, 135
Joyce, Joanne, 101
judicial branch of government, 84, 85, 87–88
Julian, Percy, 73, *73*

Kemp, Shawn, 77
Kickapoo people, 30
Kinnear, Greg, 135
Knight, Bobby, 77
Knox, George, 55
Kokomo, 73
Ku Klux Klan, 58, *58*

Lafayette, 36
"lake effect" snow, 15
Lake Michigan, 11, 12, 13,
    17, 21, 33, 35, 36, 49,
    52, 103, 106
Lake Shafer, 108
Lake Wawasee, 11
land area, 9, 11
languages, 30, 37, 54
Lanier, James Franklin Doughty,
    114
Lanier Mansion State Historic
    Site, 114
LaPorte, 104
LaPorte County Fair, 104
La Salle, René-Robert Cavelier,
    Sieur de, 35
laws, 48, 81, 84, 86, 88
Leavenworth, 113
legislative branch of government,
    63, 84, 85, 86–87, *86*
Letterman, David, 74, *74*, 135
Levi Coffin Home, 111, *111*
Lilly, Eli, 99, *99*
Limberlost home, 109
limestone, 82, 99
Lincoln, Abraham, 88, 107, 114
Lincoln Boyhood National
    Memorial, 114, *114*
Lincoln City, 114
Lincoln, Nancy, 114
Lincoln Pioneer Village and
    Museum, 115
literature, 73, 133
Little Turtle (Miami leader),
    44–45
livestock, 60, 70, 96, 98
local government, 90–91
logistics industry, 101
Lombard, Carole, 74, 135
Long, Shelley, 135
Louisiana Territory, 35
Lugar, Richard Green, 135

Madame Walker Theatre
    Center, 55
Madison, 114
Malden, Karl, 135

manufacturing, 55, 57, 61, *94*,
    95, 96, 99, 101
maps
    agricultural, *97*
    counties, *89*
    European exploration, *34*
    Indianapolis, *82*
    interstate highways, *102*
    mining, *97*
    national parks, *22*
    Native Americans, *31*
    population density, *69*
    statehood, *47*
    territorial, *47*
    topographical, *10*
Marengo, 114
Marengo Cave National
    Landmark, 114
Marietta, *41*
marine life, 17–18, 27
Marion, 73, 74, 75, 111
Marshall, Thomas Riley, 90
mastodons, 26, *26*
Mayberry, Virginia, 61
McCormick's Creek State Park, *13*
McLaughlin, Jon, 135
McQueen, Steve, 74, 135
Medaryville, 105
Mellencamp, John, 75, 135, *135*
Mengering, Dorothy, *74*
Menno-Hof Amish/Mennonite
    Information Center, 106
Mennonites, 106
mercury, 19
Messick, Dale, 135
Metamora, 110
Miami people, 30, 37, 44
Michiana Mennonite Relief Sale,
    104
Michigan City, 14–15, 37, 49,
    54, 105
Michigan Road, 49
mining, 13, 96, *97*, 99
Mishawaka, 73
Mississippian culture, 29, *29*, 30
Mitchell, 114
Monticello, 108
Morgan, John Hunt, 51, 112
Morgan's Raiders, 51
Mound Builders, 27–29, *28*
Mount Baldy, *8*, 23
museums, 48, 52, 104, *104*,
    105, 106, 107, *107*, 109,
    110, 113, 114, 115
music, 59, 74–75, *75*, 113,
    133, 134, 135, *135*

Nappanee, 105
Nashville, 111
National New York Central
    Railroad Museum, 104
national parks, 8, 22, 41
National Road, 48–49
Native Americans, 7, 24, 25,
    27–29, *27*, 29–30, *31*, 33,
    35, 36, 37–38, 41, 43,
    44–45, *44*, *45*, 88, 109
New Albany, 115
New Harmony, 48
Newport, 50
New Whiteland, 16
Nicholson, Meredith, 73
Noblesville, 20
Northwest Indiana Symphony
    Orchestra, 75
Northwest Ordinance, 41, 46
Northwest Territory, 40, 45, *47*,
    133
Notre Dame, University of, 59,
    73, 77

Ogden Dunes, 21
Ohio River, 9, 12, 27, 29, *41*,
    43, 49, 51, 103, 112
Ohio Territory, 45
oil, 51–52
Owen, Robert, 48

Pacers basketball team, 78
Paleo-Indians, 24, 25, 26
Paoli Peaks, 115
Pauley, Jane, 74, 136, *136*
Peet, Bill, 136
Peru, 106
Peterson, Bart, 90
plant life, 16–17, 20, 107, *107*
Pollack, Sydney, 136
pollution, 18–19, 21, 23, 99
Pontiac (Ottawa leader), 38, *38*
population, 54, 63, 64, 67,
    68, 69, *69*
Porter, 106
Porter, Cole, 74, *74*
Posey, John Wesley, 70, *70*
Potawatomi people, 30, 45
pottery, 27, 29
Purdue University, 73, 77
Pyle, Ernie, 109, *109*

Quakers, 50
Quayle, Dan, 90
Quilters Hall of Fame, 75, 111,
    137

quilting, 75–76, *76*, 104, 105

railroads, 49, *49*, 51, 52, 54, 55, 104, 105, 112–113, 114
Redenbacher, Orville, 136
religion, 33, 48, 50, 75
Revolutionary War, 38–40, 44, 133
Richmond, 73, 75
Richmond Symphony Orchestra, 75
roadways, 48–49, 61, 62, 70, 75, 81, *102*
Roaring Twenties, 59
Roberts, John G., Jr., 87, *87*
Robertson, Oscar Palmer, 77, 79, *79*
Rockne, Knute, 59, *59*
Rockport, 115
Rockville, 112
Rolen, Scott, 78
Ross, Jerry, 73

Sable, Jean Baptiste Point du, 37
sand dunes, 13, 17, 21, 23
Sanders, Colonel Harland David, 136
Scholl, William M., 136
secession, 50–51
service industries, 101, *101*
settlers, *42*, 43, 46, *46*, 50
Sewall, May Wright, 136
Sharp, Zerna Addis, 136
Shawnee people, 30, 45, *45*
Shepherd, Jean, 136
Shipshewana, 76, 106
Skelton, Red, 136
skiing, 115
slavery, 36, 46, 48, 50, 70
South Bend, 35, 52, 59, 69, 73, 106–107
South Bend Chocolate Factory and Museum, 106, *106*
Southern Hills and Lowlands region, 12, 13
Spitz, Mark, 79
Splash Down Dunes Water Park, 106
sports, 53, *53*, 59, 77–79, *77*, *78*, 106, *106*, 115, 133, *133*
Spring Mill State Park, 114, *114*
Standard Oil Company, 51–52

state capital, 48, 82, *82*
state capitol, *80*, 82–83, *83*, 112
state constitution, 48, 50, 84, 86–87
state flag, 92, *92*
statehood, 7, 48, 93
state name, 7
state nicknames, 49, 51, 70
state parks, *13*, 27, 111, *111*, 112, *112*, 114, *114*
state seal, 93, *93*
St. Clair, Arthur, 41
Steele, Theodore Clement, 111, 136
steel manufacturing, 52, 54, 61, 64
Stephenson, David Curtis, 58
Stewart, Tony, 79, 136, *136*
Stewart, George P., 137
Stratton-Porter, Gene, 73, 109, 137
Studebaker Manufacturing Company, 52–53, 64, 107, *107*
Studebaker National Museum, 107, *107*
suburbs, 62
Sunday, Billy, 107

Taltree Arboretum & Gardens, 107, *107*
Tarkington, Booth, 137
T. C. Steele State Historic Site, 111
Tecumseh (Shawnee leader), 45, *45*
Terre Haute, 52
Tharp, Twyla, 75, 137, *137*
Till Plains region, 12, 13
Topeka, 107
tornadoes, 15–16, *15*
tourism, 100
town courts, 88
transportation, 36, 48–49, *49*, 51, 52, 59, *59*, 62, 75, 99, 101, 112
Treaty of Greenville, 45
Turkey Foot (Algonquian leader), 45
Turkey Run State Park, 112, *112*
Tuskegee Airmen, 61
Twin Swamps Nature Preserve, 16–17

Underground Railroad, 50, 111

United States Grand Prix, 100
United States Steel Corporation, 52
urban development, 20, *20*, 21

Valparaiso, 107
VanDerveer, Tara, 78, *78*
Village at Winona, 107
Vincennes, 36, 38, *39*, 41, 45, 48, 115
Vincennes State Historic Sites, 115
Vonnegut, Kurt, Jr., 137
Voss, Janice E., 73
voting rights, 48, 136

Wabash River, 9, 11, 12, 27, 29, 36, 41, 42, 43, 48
Walker, Charles D., 73
Walker, Madam C. J., 55, *55*
Wallace, Lew, 137
Waller, Fats, 59
War of 1812, 45
Warren, Michael, 137, *137*
Washington, George, 44
Washington Park Zoo, 105, *105*
Wayne, Anthony, 44
Webster, Marie D., 75, 111, 137
West Baden Springs, 112–113
West Baden Springs Hotel, 113
West Beach, *8*
West, Jessamyn, 137
wetlands, 17, 107
White River, 48
White, Ryan, 137
Whitewater Canal State Historic Site, 110
Whitewater River, 15
Whiting, 52, 55
wildlife. *See* animal life; insect life; marine life; plant life.
Williams, Donald, 73
Winona Lake, 107
Wise, Robert, 137
Wolf, David, 73
Works Progress Administration (WPA), 61
World War I, 55, 57, 58
World War II, 61, 63, 109, 134
Wright, Wilbur, 137
Wyandotte Caves, 113, *113*

Zoeller, Frank "Fuzzy," 137

AUTHOR'S TIPS AND SOURCE NOTES

★ ★ ★

A lot of credit for preserving the Hoosier heritage goes to the Indiana Historical Society in Indianapolis. Its online materials, reading recommendations, and publications, such as *Indiana: A New Historical Guide* by Robert M. Taylor Jr., have been very valuable in researching this book. Other books, such as *Indiana Trivia* by Ernie and Jill Couch and *Oddball Indiana* by Jerome Pohlen, have provided facts on the lighter side. The Michigan City Public Library has a wealth of information about the German immigrants who came to the area in the 1800s. Finally, much thanks goes to helpful Hoosiers, such as the folks at the statehouse and in the office of the Indianapolis mayor, who took the time to answer my questions and help me fill in the blanks.